Also by

Marisa P. Moris

and

Joseph P. Moris

Answers – Heaven Speaks

Conversations with Jesus and the New Testament Authors

The Bible Speaks

Conversations with Jesus
and the New Testament Authors

Book I

Featuring

Matthew and Mark

By

Joseph P. Moris
Marisa P. Moris

The Bible Speaks   Book I   Featuring Matthew and Mark

This book is dedicated to
Jesus **Yeshua** Christ
and all those up there who believe in this journey

Conversations with Jesus and the New Testament Authors

The Bible Speaks

Copyright © 2015
by
Joseph P. Moris and Marisa P. Moris

Published by Intuition Publishing

Printed in the United States of America
ISBN 978-0-9898851-2-6

Intuition Publishing
1054 2nd Street
Encinitas, CA 92024

info@discoverintuition.com

Format and Cover by Roger C. Bull
Edited by Joseph Moris
Cover Photo by Joseph Moris off the Carlsbad California
Coastline at Terramar

All rights reserved. The contents of this book may not be reproduced in any form, except for short extracts for quotation or review, without the written permission of the publisher.

The Bible Speaks Book I Featuring Matthew and Mark

© Joseph P Moris and Marisa P Moris
First Published by Intuition Publishing
ISBN 978-0-9898851-2-6

All rights Reserved.
The contents of this book may not be reproduced in any form, except for short extracts for quotation or review, without the written permission of the publisher.

Intuition Publishing
1054 2nd Street
Encinitas, CA 92024

info@discoverintuition.com

Transcriptions by Monica Harris
Printed in the United States of America
First Edition: November 2015

20 19 18 17 16 15 14 13 12 11

Library of Congress Cataloging-in-Publication Data

The Bible Speaks
Joseph P Moris and Marisa P Moris
p.   cm.
ISBN 978-0-9898851-0-2

Table of Contents

Introduction to Matthew and Mark: *7*
Foreword: *13*
Chapter 1:   *Introduction to Matthew and Jesus*   *14*
Chapter 2:   *Interview with Matthew*   *21*
Chapter 3:   *Matthew and Who is Rosemary?*   *57*
Chapter 4:   *Interview with Mark*   *98*
Authors: *157*

Introduction to Matthew and Mark

In our first book, Answers Heaven Speaks (hereafter *Heaven Speaks*) Marisa and I introduced ourselves, our stories and how we've ended up where we are today.

In summary Marisa is a clear channel clairvoyant who was never religious by nature or design. I became a born again Christian in 1998. Marisa is not a psychic or fortune teller; she is someone who in 2009 had a near death experience, spoke to a very recognizable angel on the "other side" and was told it wasn't yet her time to go. Marisa was upset that she couldn't stay in heaven and after coming back to this world she began a journey of education. She was bound and determined in trying to learn, short of killing herself, how to come face to face again with the angel that told her it wasn't her time yet to die. The angel looked just like Marisa but she was huge and so "spiritual" and peaceful in nature. The word "spiritual" at that point in Marisa's life was not a word that was widely used or found in her vocabulary.

But, on Easter morning of 2010 and after much study, like an epiphany Marisa realized who Christ was and who Jesus was. She then, through her tears proceeded to baptize herself right then and there in her bathtub. Following that experience along with additional study into the Eastern Arts, Marisa found herself able to channel. It wasn't long before she was able to communicate with guides, angels and teachers from the "other side".

Now, over the last several years Marisa has become a very clear channel to everything from past loved ones to Christ himself and so much in between. Marisa could have run off to the dark side with her special abilities but chose instead to work strictly in the "light"….the "light of Christ".

Heaven Speaks was an introduction to what we learned from the other side about the usual questions by seekers of truth. Who are we, why are we here and what the heck is life all about. After addressing those issues, we concluded in the Epilogue that our next book would be about the Earth's Mysteries. The Pyramids and UFOs have always fascinated me.

So in Marisa's abilities I saw opportunities to ask, ask and ask some more about the earth's mysteries. I was quite anxious to learn some of these mysteries so that was going to be the main focus of our second book. But in order to understand the earth's mysteries, we also felt that the vast unexplained mysteries of the universe were also needing to be touched upon as well; for we've come to learn that in addition to the earth's mysteries there are mysteries of the universe that are just as intriguing, such as the "administration" of the universe and the structure of the soul and the structure of the dimensions. These are just two of the countless mysteries of the universe(s)....not to mention that we don't even know how many universes there are; for that could very well be an infinite number. While trying to grasp that little tidbit of curiosity we came to realize and understand just how small we are in this vast universe and yet on this little earth, how close we are to the spiritual world.

It's all so mind boggling to comprehend but Marisa and I eventually sat down in early 2014, turned on the recorder again, said a prayer requesting protection from evil and then commenced by asking the "other side" about the earth's various world-wide pyramids. Numerous visitors come in to teach us about these phenomena. The channeling session was nearly two hours long. During the session I can remember thinking just how fascinating and intriguing the information we were being taught was. But, I was also coming to believe that there wouldn't be very many open-minded people on this earth who would believe what we were learning. I was in a state of quandary as to what to do. Neither Marisa nor I wanted to end up with a book so equally simple and yet so complex that it would be considered fiction or nonsense.

So, at the end of that first taped session into all kinds of mysteries, mainly about the earth, and with a heavy head about the credibility of the information we had just been presented with, and how we were going to present it ourselves, in frustration I asked Marisa if she was able to ask Jesus a question. We had had many sessions putting together our first book *Heaven Speaks* but we never gave much thought to ask Jesus into one of them (he has since told us that he attended every one of the sessions and at times came in looking and speaking like someone Marisa felt comfortable speaking with).

When Jesus appeared to Marisa we were both stunned. Nevertheless, I asked Jesus an innocuous question as to whether Paul, the biblical author of thirteen books of the New Testament, wrote his thirteen epistles from his heart or by visions or by visitations of angels? I asked "What and how did Paul write what theologians today call 'God's Words'"? Jesus responded by saying "ask him yourself". At that point Paul appeared to Marisa. After asking Paul the question and following his answer I exclaimed to Marisa how cool it would be to interview Jesus' apostles. Upon further consideration it made more sense to interview the authors of the New Testament instead as the majority of Christians wouldn't necessarily be familiar with the epistles of the apostles Andrew, Philip, Thomas, Bartholomew and others but we felt that they would recognize the names of Matthew, Mark, Luke, John, James, Jude and Paul; the New Testament Authors.

When I told Marisa that I would really enjoy interviewing the Authors of the New Testament she was less than enthusiastic. In fact, she thought it was pretty lame and stupid. You have to understand that Marisa knew about as much about the Bible as I knew about the way females think; which is virtually nothing. She was sure she would muck these interviews up somehow but to both of our surprises, the results turned out to be awe inspiring instead.

What follows in this book and the succeeding books dedicated to the individual New Testament Authors (and after this series, the Old Testament) is a magical look back over 2000 years ago to the lives of those entrusted by God to be the Authors of the New Testament and what they experienced in their lives before and after meeting Jesus. The intricacies that flow from these channeled sessions bring a curiosity and are nothing short of mind boggling, exciting and fun.

The interviews with these authors are broken down "two by two" into a five book series. There are eight authors so there are Books I-IV with the authors and a Book V that will be a one-on-one with Jesus. We don't have to wait through four books to hear from Jesus though. On the contrary, Jesus has and does moderate all the way through these series of interviews so we get a great idea of who Jesus was then and still is today.

Almost everyone we know (I am a devout church goer and Marisa is a Master Certified Reiki Instructor) worries that communicating with the "other side" is the work of Satan and Lucifer. Even I feared that we were headed in a dangerous direction in the beginning of our interviews but after considerable prayer and faith in Christ we went on to discuss that further in *Heaven Speaks*. We are thoroughly convinced now that the lessons that we have learned in these interview sessions could only have come from God...not from the dark side. We are a thousand percent sure of that. There is no way a reader can come away from these books feeling like they were being deceived by the dark side. Glorifying God is not one of Lucifer's strong points.

The effect of learning the personalities of these historical authors brings new substance when reading their scriptures. There is a sense now of actually being there in their midst while you read their words. Reading scripture is so much more interesting and understandable now. The education we've received and are passing along within these covers will help you to better understand the authors immensely.

It is so much fun getting to know the "characters" of *The Bible Speaks;* for as you come to know the characters better it will also help you to learn not only more about them but more about yourself as well. Jesus gives us several new 21st century parables as well. Jesus makes things so simple with his examples. In *Heaven Speaks* many times you will find the words "quantum physics" in the same sentence as "kindergarten". In our first book it was our goal to bring what seemed like quantum physics down to a simple math level. In his brilliance Jesus goes one step further with his examples and parables. He makes something akin to quantum physics simple enough that a kindergarten child could actually understand. The following series of books on the authors also brings many complicated spiritual matters down to a simple math as well. What seemed so difficult to grasp prior to reading these personal accounts of the authors becomes so much more understandable now and the new parables that Jesus introduces explain his points so effortlessly.

Marisa and I have learned so much! We've definitely learned just how real God is. We've become friends with Jesus and we've been taught the role of "angels" in our lives. They're not really all angels. It is just much simpler to address those spirits on the other side as angels even though they call themselves something entirely different. They call themselves guides and teachers and such but to me, they're all angels. Everyone we've met on the other side is very real. Unfortunately though, the underworld and evil are just as real so we used great caution in our prayers and protection to keep evil away from our sessions. The authors have further taught us how evil and misery can be overcome through the understanding of who we really are and from where we came.

What is really cool is that Jesus further told us that as the readers read his words in these texts Jesus will be right there with them. He even told us that each of the characters in these books will also be with the reader when these other characters come to life within the pages. Just think about that for a moment. Just imagine that while you are reading their words, the spirit of that character will literally be sitting right there next to you. You will become infused with that spirit's energy while you read his or her words. You should also be able to take note of the feelings of peace that will envelope you as you come to know each of the participants in these books as well.

We did not dissect or try to analyze passages from the New Testament books. We took a peek at what made these Authors tick instead. We wanted to get to know the person, not just the words of the person. So, as you embark on this great discovery you will find that God and his administration are so much more than you could have ever imagined.

Those Christians who are comfortable in their faith will find these books to be quite supportive of their instinctual love for God and Jesus Christ. And, readers who call themselves Christians but are not really sure why and could be better labeled as "seekers" instead will find through their curiosity just how profound the Holy Spirit is, who God is, who Jesus was and still is today.

The authors have told us that these books about themselves will fill a burning curiosity. There is a curiosity among believers that longs to be right there with Jesus when he walked the earth; what it might have been like to have walked with him and his apostles oh so long ago. And, to learn what kind of men and women Jesus/Yeshua felt a kinship toward that they would end up in his inner circle.

These interviews really blew me away. It was and continues to be very humbling to have had this opportunity and therefore Marisa and I both hope you will experience a similar awakening and fulfillment of this curiosity. Each and every reader will interpret and react to the following words/pages/chapters in different ways but to each it will be a journey worth the effort.

Foreword

Open your mind to what might be. Open your mind and spirit to Christ and see if these accounts will give you the understanding of just who these men and women were that were so lucky to have spent portions of their lives in the presence of God....even if Jesus never said he was God. Let's just jump in and see what Matthew and Mark were all about.

Both of these men had a history before meeting Jesus and it was those life experiences that allowed them to grow once they were exposed to Christ and the Holy Spirit. You will have fun getting to know these guys for who they really were.

Marisa and I taped the initial interviews. Then at a later date, after having the conversations transcribed, I read back the transcriptions to them. "They" would either let it ride or add to the conversation....especially if there was a need for further clarification. (The bold print comes as clarifications, additions and corrections to the initial interviews.)

I hope you come to have a new found appreciation for Matthew and Mark. Please try to overlook perceived grammatical errors as we chose to print the words exactly the way they were given to us.

So, God Bless and enjoy!

Chapter 1

Introduction to Matthew with comments from Jesus

Recorded in April 2014

Joe: Well, if we get the OK from Jesus, we're going to start right away with Matthew; Matthew and then with Mark.

Marisa: He (Jesus) says yes.....Okay. So... calling in Matthew; will you let Matthew come in? Matthew is not coming in. Hold on here's Jesus.

Joe: I thought he'd come (Matthew).

Marisa: Paul is here now and he was here earlier too. Are we allowed to talk to Matthew?

(asking Jesus or anyone else up there willing to listen and respond)

(Jesus) My son, my daughter, please understand this and understand while as you bring in these vibrations, these high vibrating souls, you may bring one in at a time for you have many souls in this room and the vibration in which you carry is not high enough to connect with each

of those, for you must ask Paul to take a step out so that Matthew may enter.

Marisa: Okay, so Paul, can you like wait on the bench or something? I'm treating him like a second string fielder.

Joe: Paul's going to be a big interview, because he has 13 books. Paul is not one of the original twelve apostles. He became a self-proclaimed apostle when he went out teaching about Jesus, the Christ.

Marisa: Oh, okay. – so who's another one? Like Samuel or – or Michael or who's another one?

Joe: There are Matthew, Mark, and Luke.

Marisa: Okay. So can Mark and Matthew be in the room at the same time?

(Jesus) Yes.

Joe: I'm just curious. I want to learn the lives of these authors. So I'm going to be asking – you know, I'm going to be asking them questions that I would ask somebody today. You know, what was your life like when you were growing up? What were your parents like? Et cetera.

Marisa: Okay. Let's see if they answer.

Joe: And then we'll eventually get to Jesus.

Marisa: All right. Well, Jesus wants to give us a message

Joe: Great.

Marisa: He says that there's a piece of him that can communicate with anybody on the earth plane, because that's why he made himself available through the Holy Spirit. The Holy Spirit is like a little internal GPS honing device. It's like a little walkie-talkie that can communicate with him. And even if they're down in the depths of hell, whether they're on the earth plane or in the ethers of the astral plane, they can still call out for his help and be forgiven. The problem with the ones on the lower planes is they think they'll be judged so they don't call Jesus for help.

[(Jesus) **"And this is true. This is true my child, this is true my brother, my sister. But what one must understand and be able to differentiate is that with the Holy Spirit, with this beacon of light that each carries within them, they can communicate with God, they can communicate with their soul, they can communicate with anything that has a Holy Spirit, which is everything. So this is not just a way to communicate with me, which this may have come through as the Holy Spirit is a way to communicate with only me. The Holy Spirit is what this channel is using to communicate with that which is this side, as you call it, the "other side" (and everything in it). The Holy Spirit is the walkie-talkie within each human being that can communicate with the upper realms."*]*

Marisa: So he's saying that he can lower his vibration so that he can channel – I can channel him. Okay, so let's see – oh, I didn't finish the prayer. Let's see here. Okay.

Someone named Rosemary is here from the Bible. I don't know this Rosemary. She said she lived back then. Mother Mary (is here) and John the Baptist is standing right behind Papa.

Joe: Wow.

Marisa: *So, thank you God, for giving us these Ascended Masters to work with us tonight. And, please, please, please help me to not be nervous and to not block any of the information in which they're bringing throughout (my) insecurity or fear of being wrong. This is one of my downfalls, not wanting to be wrong, and I ask that you lift this from me, at least for this short amount of time and over the next couple of hours. Also, (I'm) calling in Jesus, the aspect of Jesus that I'm able to communicate with and (asking Joe) – who did you want? Mark? Luke? So, calling in all of the -- all of the angels and the Elohim and any guides that I have that make me a clear channel; just come in now but only as long as you're for my highest and best good. I prefer the Ascended Masters, but if I have another guide……calling in Samuel. Alright, thank you Father, amen.*

Joe: *Well, hopefully Paul isn't taking this personally – well, they don't have human emotions on the other side.*

Marisa: *They don't. No.*

Joe: *So he's not taking it personally that we're putting him off for a little while is he because, I've got a lot of questions for Paul?*

Marisa: *No, they don't take anything personally. Let's see. Do you guys take anything personally? I can't see*

Matthew. I can just sense him. Well here, let's – let me get you Jesus real quick so . . .

Joe: Jesus wanted to tell us about.....

Marisa: Yeah. I wanted to finish the prayer and make sure it was really Jesus. So the prayer's done. All right Jesus, you can step into my energy. Are you communicating with me, or are you communicating with my higher self? Communicating with me? You're channeling through me?

(Jesus) No. Through your higher self yes.

Marisa: Okay. All right I Just needed to know who I need to be listening to. My higher self is the one that always says "what we would like to say is.....". So my higher self is the translator between Jesus and me right now, just to make that clear. I'm not actually channeling Jesus I'm channeling my higher self who's channeling Jesus.

Joe: Okay, but is Matthew here?

Marisa: Yeah. He's over in the corner. He's got like a –

Joe: ...well, let's ask him if we can have permission to talk to him.

Marisa: With him? Well, we're talking – Jesus is trying to talk.

Joe: Okay.

Marisa: Matthew is sitting on a log poking a fire with a stick. Just like – who's Rosemary? Is there a Rosemary in the Bible?

Joe: Not that I know of.

Marisa: Who's this Rosemary lady then? I think its Rosemary.

Joe: There's a Ruth. Ruth was Jesus's sister.

Marisa: No, it's not Ruth. It's like Rosio or Rose or – oh, well. It's doesn't matter. She's over there standing kind of in the corner. Are you from the Bible times? She says yes. She traveled with the – with the pack of people.

Joe: Oh, she was probably one of the women disciples.

Marisa: She says she wasn't a disciple. She was a wife.

Joe: Oh? A wife of whom?

Marisa: Wife of – I just heard a wife of John.

Joe: It's possible. John never spoke of a wife in his epistles.

Marisa: Was it the John that wrote the books in the Bible? She says yes. Wait. Were you his wife or his daughter?

(Rosemary) Neither.

Marisa: Were you guys like really married, or were you like boyfriend/girlfriend? She says it's more like a companionship, boyfriend/girlfriend type thing. She –

they were like great friends. Okay, well, hold on one second. Let's talk to Jesus first and then we'll get some hearsay from the self-proclaimed girlfriend.

Joe: Okay.

Chapter 2

Interview with Matthew

Well, that was an interesting opening to Matthew. He was tougher to communicate with than we thought. Nevertheless, here we go. This interview could be as spotty as the previous chapter but you will still get to know Matthew better....we promise.

Recorded April 2014

Joe: Well, let's get started. Let's see if Matthew is ready to go. If Matthew's ready, I'm just going to ask questions —

Marisa: Okay. Was Matthew noble or rich?

Joe: He was probably rich because he was a tax collector.

Marisa: Because he's wearing – he's wearing his fancy robes and kind of like poking at the fire.

Joe: Are they like velvet-type robes or are they like burlap-type robes?

Marisa: Burlap.

Joe: Really. Hmmmm...

Marisa: Yeah. It's kind of like what you see the monks wear... sort of like the brown burlap robes but underneath he's showing me that he's wearing like a – it's like – I don't know...he's really wearing something underneath or it's just imagery, but it's like red and blue with the buttons and it goes up to his neck. So it's like he's showing me that he's – that he had some money or something underneath, so he's showing that –

Joe: That's probably symbolism.

Marisa: Yeah. It's like – it looks like he has coins right here, like gold coins but it's kind of like those people that stand with their elbow bent like royalty and he's showing me that he believed he was royalty in his own ego, in his own mind. Let me see here. He's poking the fire and he's thinking back to who he was.

Joe: I want to go back to the beginning. I want to learn about his childhood. I want to find out some things. I'd like to find out what his mom and dad were like, what it was like growing up. First off, trying to figure out why he became a tax collector, so I'd like to know what his mom and his dad were like first and then let's go from there. What were his mom and dad like? What kind of people were they? Were they harsh on him as a child? Were they patient with him as a child? Demanding? Were both parents there with him throughout his life?

Marisa: Okay, hold on. Let me see. **[He says that's incorrect. He didn't think he was royalty in his own ego.]**

(Matthew) "The mother in whom I had was far out of the picture in terms of emotional stability. The father in whom I had was like any other father (at that time) for they were not necessarily cruel. They had a heavy hand in keeping the kids schooled and in line. Just as any, just as any human being at that time, the conscious level was much lower so the savagery, the savagery of eat, sleep, mate, protect one's lives, ran much higher for growing up and the understanding that money was the only thing that kept us unhappy. This is the image in which I saw. The only thing I wanted to do was to make money to make myself unhappy."

Joe: To make himself unhappy or happy by making money?

(Matthew) I was used to being unhappy –

Marisa: Hold on a second.   Someone is jumping in. Who's Rosemary?

Joe: *I have no idea.   Maybe she came* –

Marisa: Can Rosemary – can you take a step out of here? I don't know who you are, and unless you tell me who you are, you can't stay. Okay. She's coming to sit over here. Okay. He's saying that – that he saw money as something that was – that was the only thing that was keeping them from being happy and that when he grew up he wanted to make money so that he could take care of his family and be – and keep himself from being unhappy so he wanted – he thought it would make him happy, but through ridicule and the names and the harshness that came from everybody from being what he was, it basically made him unhappy and so in turning his life *over* (to God through Jesus) *the relief was lifted and that in itself changed him.*

Joe: Well, I don't want to get right up to the point of him meeting Jesus yet. I'm going to want to know what his thoughts and feelings were. In the Bible itself, he's somewhat a legalistic person, kind of with a heavy hand, a strong Jew and – so that must come from his parents' upbringing. I know that in those days the mother would usually drop out of boys lives at the age of 12 and then the father takes over. How many brothers and sisters did he have?

(Matthew) Seven.

Joe: Was he the oldest, youngest, in the middle?

(Matthew) Fourth.

Joe: He was number 4? Middle child tends to get neglected somewhat. They find their own path. They tend to be stronger people because they have to fight their way along. They don't find –

Marisa: He says he wasn't....he always felt less than....he always felt ignored and let the others be strong until he was 14.

Joe: What happened at 14?

Marisa: He says he fell in love.

Joe: He fell in love?

Marisa: He says he fell in love. He liked the girl. He thought he was in love and he decided that he needed to be something different than what he was.

Joe: What was he? Was he shy? Quiet?

Marisa: Yeah. He's saying he was – he wouldn't call it shy. He would just call it withdrawn....withdrawn.

Joe: Did the girl he fell in love with end up becoming his wife?

Marisa: No.

Joe: It was just his first love?

Marisa: His first. He says as you would say in this lifetime, in this part of the timeline in which he lived, it was a first crush.

Joe: Puppy love.

Marisa: In wanting to be noticed.

Joe: Did she hurt him?

Marisa: No. She never even knew he existed.

Joe: Oh, okay. That's so much like teenagers today.

Marisa: Yes. Human beings do not change.

Joe: Did he continue in school? Did he get some kind of what we would call a degree?

(Matthew) What you would call 8th Grade.

Joe: He went as far as 8th Grade?

(Matthew) But that's a much higher level than anyone else would be going through for most boys would be sent off, sent off to work in mills, sent off to work in farms, sent off to work by the age of what you would say 2nd Grade.

Joe: Oh. Based on their intelligence? In other words, those who showed promise to learn, to be able to read and write would continue on through school whereas those who didn't – I mean, it sounds –

(Matthew) My father felt it was important to be schooled for he saw and spoke of those who were schooled as having more money. He was the one that placed the importance on if we had more money we would be happy. So I aimed to please and I was not one of the very strong ones. I had brothers who were very strong that felt that the aspects of themselves were better for them to basically go to work doing hard labor.

Joe: So he was more of a cerebral person than a physical person.

Marisa: Yes.

Joe: Did he consider himself a religious person? Did he find being a Jew and learning the Torah and the other books of the Old Testament cumbersome or did that spark the light of God in him? There's a reason why I'm asking that because he did become a tax collector and to me it would seem like a tax collector would be a cynical type of person.

(Matthew) It's the understanding that there's one God. There are many people at this time that believed in more gods.

Joe: *What was his feeling?*

(Matthew) My mother believed in more gods but did not speak of this for the curiosity that I had of the multiple gods was something that was there. Just (as they) say you two are curious. But it was never spoken of. And know that there was no light stricken within from the religion in which we are born into for we did not truly understand. All we knew was God would kill us if we were bad.

Joe: *So they feared God.*

(Matthew) Yes and fear of the church too. I felt that by becoming a tax collector, by becoming something of power, I was becoming powerful and noticed, for all that was built on anger though.

Joe: *How did he become a tax collector? Did he have to pass a test? Did he have to learn how to fight better?*

(Matthew) There was a man in the village in which we sold our goods that came, came when I was 17 and spoke of this. Becoming a tax collector was something that, as you would say, had to go through the government. This is not something that you could just become. I felt as if it was an opportunity that I could not pass up and my father encouraged it (but) very shortly after, he died.

Joe: *About how old was his dad when he died?*

(Matthew) He was in his early 50's. He was a very hard working, what you would call today, a range hand. His hands were always rough.

[(Matthew) "So, when I became a tax collector and among the wealthy, looking back now I was so proud that my hands were not rough. But I didn't feel and wasn't able to give the love of a soft heart like my father because, unlike his hands, my heart became rough instead. One of my teachings that I brought is that it is what is inside that is what counts, not the outside."]

Joe: That was a good – pretty good long life back then?

Marisa: Actually he just said 43.

Joe: 43?

Marisa: Wait. Rosemary, who are you?

Joe: Matthew, do you know who this Rosemary is that keeps popping in?

Marisa: He says no. Who do you belong with? Who's Chris? Okay. You guys, just go

Joe: So at 17 he found a mentor who can –

Marisa: A mentor found him.

Joe: The mentor found him?

Marisa: Uh-huh. He saw that Matthew was easy to train or – he says now looking back, brainwash.

Joe: Okay. That makes sense. Why is it that he seemed to stand out? Was it because he was a loner or because he was highly social? Was Matthew highly social? What I'm trying to figure out is what made Matthew tick.

Marisa: Seeing Matthew – okay, Matthew. Step into my energy please. I don't want a lower human Matthew, I want a higher Matthew. Maybe the other – the spirits are coming in because we're talking to the lower aspects of them. Matthew says his writings are completely changed.

Joe: Again, I don't want to pull anybody from their faith or their love of the Bible, but we're going to be interviewing everyone. I'm sure everyone feels that their work was toyed with by Constantine and his council. Is that the case, Matthew? Did Constantine change or skew your epistles? Your letters?

(Matthew) "Not him directly. There were scribes that took these writings and changed them."

Joe: I don't want to go in that direction right now for we can get into that a little bit later. How long were you a tax collector?

Marisa: Twelve years.

Joe: Before Jesus came into your life were you ever introduced to Jesus?

(Matthew) It was already twelve years that I was a tax collector and I knew of Jesus.

Joe: Who brought Jesus to your attention? According to our Bible, you were the one chosen by Jesus to become a disciple and an apostle, so you obviously met him before he became world-renowned, before he became known as the Son of Man, the Son of God.

Marisa: He's saying again that he was a tax collector for 11 years and 8 months from the age of 23 before meeting Jesus. Okay, so you were mentored by this person that was brought into your life. Was that person brought into your life so that you can become a tax collector so that you could later repent?

(Matthew) Yes. This was the plan.

Marisa: Okay. So you planned that before you incarnated?

(Matthew) "Yes."

Marisa: Was that a guide that mentored you, by the Divine?

(Matthew) "Yes."

Marisa: Okay. So Jesus, Jesus came into his life at 11 years into his profession. He knew of Jesus 8 months prior to not being a tax collector any more....

Joe: Who met who?

Marisa: Jesus walked up to him.

Joe: What was his first impression of Jesus?

(Matthew) He was just a regular guy.

Joe: Was Jesus an outwardly friendly smiling man or was he –

(Matthew) He was quiet. He smiled. I, being the person I was, always trying to impress, thought he was being fake. I didn't believe all the stories that were told because I was surrounded by my own envy, anger and frustration.

Joe: Was he there when John the Baptist, baptized Jesus?

(Matthew) No.

Joe: Okay. Did he meet Jesus after Jesus was baptized by John....

(Matthew) Before.

Joe: So there must have been some scuttle in the community then that there was something special about Jesus.

(Matthew) Yes. Everybody spoke of Jesus from the time that Jesus was born, but then Jesus was nowhere around.

Joe: Where was he?

(Matthew) He reemerged, reemerged into the city into which he was born and there were stories, stories of a prophet, stories of a messiah.

Joe: Before he was baptized?

(Matthew) Yes.

Joe: And before he even met him?

(Matthew) Yes. There were –

Joe: So you were cynical when you met him. He was a smiling, friendly guy, but you were disbelieving of some of the stories.

(Matthew) Absolutely.

Joe: Why? What was drawing you to him then? Is it just because of a hardened heart being a tax collector and everybody hated you as a tax collector?

(Matthew) I believed that money was God.

[Marisa: He keeps talking about, and I don't know if he gets back into this, but he says he met Jesus when he was first a tax collector. Like, just kind of like a run-in type thing. That's what he's talking about right now. But he "met him" met him, and knew him three years before he quit as a tax collector. So what he's saying is there is a big gap there. It was kind of one of those passersby like "Oh hey there's that guy that everybody talks about, oh look, hey, he's smiling at me, what a fake." And then he says time went by in his own world and then that's when he had some sort of run-in with Jesus and a pack of people. He wasn't the first apostle was he?

Joe: No, in fact I think he tells us he was the last.

Marisa: Yeah, there's a pack. Okay, go ahead.]

(Matthew) With all the prayers in which we said when we were young, we never had money fall from the sky. There was never money sent to us to take care of us. So when one says to put their faith in something that you cannot see, this was not something I was willing to do. So when one tries to live on faith by wives' tales and stories of hearing that someone is going to come save us, it made me upset. It was not realistic and, oh boy was I wrong.

Joe: Being as cynical as you were and even after meeting Jesus, did Jesus melt your heart upon your first meeting, or were you still continuing to be cynical and unbelieving?

(Matthew) Cynical and unbelieving.

Joe: Then what changed your heart? And how long after your first meeting with Jesus did you change your mind and decide to follow him? According to the Bible, Jesus asked you to follow him and you followed him, so we –

(Matthew) An angel appeared to me. An angel appeared to me three days after I had met him again. An angel appeared in my dream and I dreamt of an angel whose name is Raphael. Raphael came to me to say that all of the riches, all of the riches I had ever wanted, were waiting for me. I took that as I was going to be rich. This is the way my mind worked at the time and I woke up excited. I woke up and said to myself "I must do this so people will not hate me." But, oh boy, was I wrong. There were a lot of people; many people hated those of

us that followed him. And please, I prefer to call him Yeshua, not Jesus.

Joe: Okay. We'll keep it at Yeshua.

(Matthew) Thank you.

Marisa: (Asking Joe) When and who changed it to Jesus?

Joe: He was born as Yeshua Ben Joseph and somewhere along the way his name became Americanized or Englishized (sic, Anglicized) – to Jesus. I'm not sure when it was actually changed. Maybe its possible Constantine did, I'm just not sure. Well, we'll learn more. So throughout your knowledge or throughout your tenure with Yeshua, nobody called him Jesus?

(Matthew) Nobody called him Jesus.

Joe: Oh, okay. So that's our made-up name for him.

(Matthew) Yes.

Joe: So you saw an angel Raphael and you woke up excited in the morning. Was your father still alive or had he already passed on?

(Matthew) My earthly father had already passed on.

Joe: So was there anybody that you went to after you had this dream other than to Yeshua to discuss the dream?

(Matthew) I went to my brother, Paul.

Joe: We're not talking about Saul of Tarsus?

(Matthew) No.

Joe: You just had a brother by the name of Paul?

(Matthew) Yes, my brother Paul. He was two years older and I looked up to him.

Joe: What did he think? What did Paul think when...that you were going to drop being a tax collector and run off with a – with what many people were calling –

(Matthew) He was a religious man.

Joe: He was what?

(Matthew) He was a religious man. He had faith, and this is why I went to him because I thought he would believe in angels. He said to do what I felt God would not judge me for, for he feared God just as every other person did, and in his eyes he did not disobey God by any means.

Joe: So Paul felt that because of the dream you had that you should follow Jesus then, follow Yeshua.

(Matthew) My brother told me to do what I felt unjudged doing and to do that which I thought God would not judge me for. So he did not tell me one thing to do or the other. He let me make the decision.

Joe: How long after your dream did you – before you approached Yeshua?

(Matthew) He came back to me.

Joe: Oh, he already knew about the dream and Raphael the angel.

(Matthew) Yes.

Joe: So he must have asked the angel to come into your dream obviously.

(Matthew) No he didn't. The angels – the way that creation is made is it is all happening on this side. Everything is already happening and all the pieces like a chessboard are being moved around. And sometimes not even the most awakened people know what is going on behind the scenes. But this role...this story that has been told throughout human history of the virgin having a child and the child growing up and becoming enlightened in healing, in dying, in resurrecting, this is something somewhat like a play that was to be played out for human beings to understand that there is more than just them and that there is forgiveness. So there are many angels acting on this side, the "other side", to put things into motion.

Joe: Didn't you question Yeshua as to why he was welcoming you, a lowly tax collector that everybody hated?

(Matthew) No. I knew that he – if he was the Godly man that he said he was, I saw in my eyes that he felt as if he was getting good points with God by helping somebody like me.

Joe: Did he know he was God before – before his baptism, or did he just act on what he had been told by his – from his mother, from his birth?

(Matthew) He did not know he was God and never claimed to be God.

Joe: That's different than in the Bible, because in the Book of John, we know that he tells people that he is –

(Matthew) He is speaking of the spirit inside. He is not speaking of Yeshua the man. He is speaking of the incarnated spirit inside of him as he speaks with that higher aspect of himself through channeling.

Joe: (Interrupting Matthew and telling Marisa) Now remember, we need Jesus to jump in at any time here to correct anything being said.

Marisa: Yeah, he will.

(Jesus) I have an innate knowing...

Marisa: This is Jesus

(Jesus) There was an innate knowing from the time that I was born. There was an understanding that I was here to do something just as both of you understood that you are here to do something. You have always had that urge. You have always had that curiosity. You have always looked at the stars and said, "Is this really all that there is?" So you have had a knowing. You have had a knowing that these days were coming, that this time is coming, that this ministry was coming. So you did know. You do know and this is the same way that I knew that there was something, something there. This was my reason for taking my travels to India and to Egypt and to different places of the world to understand and learn the healing arts and to understand how human beings in the ancient times were able to heal themselves and to pray

for themselves and to not have to go to an intermediary between human beings and God. I learned just like every other human being learns how to associate oneself with God. I studied and I learned. This is not something where I was born and I automatically knew everything, but I did know. I did know I was on a mission.

[Marisa: Paul says --.

Joe: Which Paul? Because we're referring to Paul --.

Marisa: Paul with the red flag... Paul with the hand.]

(Authors note) References to anything Paul or Luke said or did will be covered further in the book that features Paul and Luke. Each book in the series can't help but have inclusions by other authors as well.

[Joe: Okay, this isn't Paul then, Matthew's brother Paul?

Marisa: No. This is Paul with the hand. He's over there because remember, he said he'd take the red flag.

Joe: This is the Apostle Paul then.

Marisa: Yeah. He's saying --. Hold on. Let me see.

[(Paul) There are many little things here that are a little bit off, for there are many words that are said that are brought through the channel with a smidgeon, as she would say – [he's using my brain to talk] – a smidgeon of her spots, of her beliefs. So if we were to rewind this, rewind this, going back to, going back to when Jesus and Matthew were brought together, they were brought together in a dream, so to speak. They were brought together in a dream where an angel brought them together. For, this was not a full-fledged appearance of an angel that came to Yeshua and said, "Go and meet upon this man and bring him into your ministry." This was not something like this. They were brought together in a dream just as many people on the earth plane at this time are brought together in dreams. They are brought together in the higher realms in their dream state and then meeting the next day they think, "This person looks very familiar. I feel like I've met them before." It's because they had met them the night before. And when one has mentioned that everything happens first in the astral plane, this is not true. This is not true. Many things are played out in the astral plane, many things are played out in the higher realms, but not everything happens there first for this was an incorrect statement and this is something that I wanted to correct. For many times, many times this channel has said that everything happens first in the astral plane, but one must say that sometimes things happen afterwards, for time does not exist. So as I create these words right now that I speak unto her and speak into her energy, I create these words now and speak them through, they have not happened already, and therefore are starting to happen in the physical plane. So in keeping this simple, I must say that, yes, there are some things that are wrong here and this is what, this is

what Luke was speaking of.] (note: we removed the Luke interlude here as it took us on a tangent. Much will be learned from Luke when you read Book III featuring both Paul and Luke) *[Luke was also speaking of Jesus – Luke was also speaking of the fact that he believes that Jesus knew he was God. But his beliefs are different than many of our other beliefs. Some of us believe that he thought this, for we thought this, but there was nobody that ever said or heard said that they heard him say that he was God, for he never truly said this ever, ever, never said this. So understanding and knowing that he was a very evolved soul, born into a baby boy on the earth plane during a very low consciousness level time of the earth plane, he was brought about into a world where his understanding and his belief patterns and his knowledge of the afterlife and the underworld and that of the other side, so to speak, was brought upon the earth plane with the memories held within his spirit, so to speak. So hopefully I was not scattering all the information, but I basically meant to say and to replace also, also I must say, (he cleared his throat), we do not want the birth of Jesus to appear as a play, as a play upon the earth plane. It sounds very material.]*

(Luke, we've come to know, has a very magnanimous personality. We think you'll love his story in Book III featuring him and Paul).

[(This is Luke) It sounds very material. It sounds very fake. It sounds very orchestrated. And there are many people who believe that the Jews, in order to get out of persecution of slavery, in order to be viewed differently, orchestrated a play for a man to play their savior so that people would have faith again, that something was going to save them. So we want to take this out of here.

This is what I dislike about the way that this was spoken through. I do not say that this is the channel's fault or this is the fault of those who spoke it, but it just came out in a way that I do not approve of. Not that you have to go exactly with what I approve, but this is something that I would advise against. For when you say a baby boy will be born of a virgin, will die, and will resurrect will be a play that is upon the earth plane that the people will fall for, this is a little bit of a disassociation with intelligence upon the people who believe in this. So whether this was something that was orchestrated by the divine, by the angels, by the guides, by God himself, or the Holy Spirit, it does not matter. It must be presented in a way that it was something that was of the divine and it did happen. And I do not say at this time that that is exactly what happened, for what I must say is there are many different stories behind what truly happened, but this book is not to disprove anything from the Bible, but I must say there are many things that we could say to disprove the Bible. But this is not something that we are going to do. We want to empower the people that read the Bible. We want to empower the people that read this into understanding and knowing that we were real people. We were real people with real lives, and we were not just lambs or sheep or drones following around a man who had brainwashed us into thinking that he was God, because he never claimed to be God. So just please understand and know that there are some things that are in this book that are a little bit off, but not enough off for us to come in and correct them, but this was something that I had a problem with that required my opinion.

Joe: That's good. Let's don't get too deep because I'm still going – I'm still going to interview you (Luke) later. But I appreciate you jumping in when we need explanations. I'm kind of focusing on Matthew. I want to see what kind of person would go from being a tax collector and sure of money and willing to drop that based on his trust in his brother, Paul –]

Marisa: It's not his brother, Paul. His brother, Paul, gave him advice to do what he did not feel judged doing. This is based on what the angel, the angel said.

Joe: Had he ever had a similar dream in his life?

(Matthew) Once when I was four years old, they told me I would do great things.

Joe: Well, that's great. So let's see. So now he's about 28 – no, no. He's about 34 years old. Did you have a wife and children at the time that you met Yeshua?

(Matthew) I did not.

Joe: So you're a single man. Are you a good-looking man or are you – do you think you're a good looking man, or a lady's…

(Matthew) I had women. I had women that I was with and fathered two children.

Joe: You weren't married but you fathered two children?

(Matthew) Yes.

Joe: Did you help raise those children?

(Matthew) I gave money to them, but no emotional ties.

Joe: Did that ever bother you?

(Matthew) No. Not until after, after turning over my heart, then I dealt with forgiveness, forgiveness of self.

Joe: That is a problem in the 21st century. It's very similar. There're a lot of children that don't have their father and – how did your children turn out? What did you have? Boys? Girls? Boy and a girl?

(Matthew) A boy and a girl and these women – these women would have been a disgrace to my name, disgrace to myself for they were just women that I slept with, as you would say.

Joe: Were they somehow banished from the community because they were unwed?

(Matthew) They were basically like prostitutes.

Joe: Okay. They were prostitutes. And so he –

Marisa: He was – he's showing himself with dark brown hair, like a chiseled face, really good-looking.

Joe: Matthew is good-looking?

Marisa: Yes. They're showing – they're showing him with like blue eyes – I don't know back then if they had blue eyes.

Joe: Yeah, they did.

Marisa: So like brown hair, blue eyes, kind of tanned skin. He's wearing like the noblemen's outfit sort of. You know kind of like what a prince would wear.

Joe: So he's kind of an imposing figure? Is he tall? Short?

Marisa: He's about medium build. I'd say about kind of like your height – no. He's probably like maybe like an inch shorter than Jeff (Marisa's husband). Jeff's what? Six, one or something?

Joe: He's about six foot.

Marisa: About six foot. Thin, but not like really thin – I mean he's – he's built to a certain extent, but I'd say more like naturally thin. And his shoulders are broad.

Joe: In the Bible – and just to go off in a little bit of different subject – in the Bible, Judas is the disciple, the apostle that apparently was in charge of the money. And I find that a little curious, because I would have guessed that you, Matthew, would have been the one that would have been in charge of raising funds to keep Yeshua's ministry alive so that you could eat. Is that true? Did you help Judas? Was Judas the one to handle all the money or –

(Matthew) Judas was the one that handled it.

Joe: How about Andrew? In the Urantia book, Andrew was – was like – almost like a little father to everybody. Did you look upon Andrew that way?

(Matthew) No. We all looked at each other as brothers and sisters.

Joe: Were there any hard feelings between any of you or jealousies or envy between you and any of the other apostles?

(Matthew) The only time jealousies and envies came in is when there were women, women in the picture and there were a couple that liked the same women. But this was quickly – this was quickly forgiven and banished from the group. They didn't realize that there was a greater picture.

Joe: Your times are so much different than ours here in the 21st century so it's hard obviously to relate, but . . .was Jesus okay – well, let me back up for a second. You mentioned women came into the picture. In the 21st century, think of Yeshua as a rock star and think of his apostles as the accompanying musicians and singers in his group. In the 21st century there will be groupies, we call groupies being girls and of course, you know guys follow as well, but lots and lots of girls. Did Jesus's – it's hard to use the word "fame" but his reputation—did it cause women to just fall at your feet?

(Matthew) Not at my feet, but at his. For I carried a reputation, I carried a reputation that was never fully able to be put out.

Joe: And that reputation was as the tax collector?

(Matthew) And also as the one that would abandon their child.

Joe: Oh, as a womanizer.

(Matthew) Yes.

Joe: But you changed your ways after you joined with Yeshua, correct?

(Matthew) Yes. But there is an understanding that one carries and looking back it's not that everybody spoke of this. It is – was the feeling inside of myself that I put out, that I do not deserve to have love, because I was never truly loved by my mother. I was always punished by my father. I felt money was the most important thing in order to bring me happiness. And then when being disarmed of my money, so to speak, I reverted back to that 8-year-old child that felt that I did not deserve love and needed to be punished. But Yeshua, Yeshua taught us how to release these fears and angers and energies from our field so that we may be forgiven and that we are allowed to forgive ourselves as well. I did not believe what he was saying and what he was teaching until I began to have visions myself.

Joe: How long had you been with Yeshua before you started having visions other than the initial angel in your sleep?

(Matthew) About four-and-a-half months, as you would say, four-and-a-half months is five moons.

Joe: After joining with Yeshua?

(Matthew) Yes.

Joe: And you saw – you are starting to see the other – well, what we call the "other side", you were seeing lords or angels?

(Matthew) No, not necessarily. I was seeing things that were going to be happening – happening on the earth plane and they were being delivered by someone who looked like myself as you two would call –

(Jesus interceding) this is Jesus – as you two would call the Higher Self...the "big" Matthew in heaven. And it was during his dreams that his higher self would just step in.

Marisa: Hold on. His higher self? I think it's going to be easier to talk to. He's saying –

Joe: Matthew's higher self?

Marisa: Yeah. The lower one is so boring.

Joe: Well, here's – well, you know that's kind of the way we get the portrayal of Matthew because he's the first one, he's the first book and he's very legalistic.

Marisa: Yeah, he's like so boring, he's going to put me to sleep. He's like, "yeah, whatever. Yeah, I did this." It's like, come on, dude. You're like – like you need to spice things up a little bit. The higher self (of Matthew) is saying that the life that he lived was one of pain and agony that was self-imposed and that's the reason why he went down – the reason why he went down in that lifetime was to experience the pain just as we plan to experience pain like I did. But it was a – it was something – basically self-imposed. He could have been loved like the other kids that were loved, but he isolated himself into not love and this is what – hold on...let Matthew's "big" Matthew tell it....

(Matthew's Higher Self) *We planned this life, we planned this life so that, so that this aspect of me that was, that was this apostle as you say, that this piece of me would fall into the category of what the play or the portrayal or the movie as you would say would need to play out on the earth plane so that human beings could see this recital of – of information coming through yet again, yet again as it did through history in understanding that there is something much greater than them in that God was not vengeful and evil and God did not judge. There are too many times, too many times in history and still the people feel as if God is going to kill them or strike them down, and when bad things happen they say it's because God did these things and this is all driven by fear. Matthew came down, Matthew came down to show the personification of an unhappy man bringing about irritation, depression and sadness upon himself and taking it out on others around him by loving and abandoning children and by loving money over human beings. And this was not to say that he was not – he was not the only one that loved money over human beings. Everybody loved money over human beings because this is how this – these people worked. He just happened to fall into the category of getting this money. But much of the money that he got was paid out to many other people so the amount of money that he was actually keeping was not as much as he thought it would or should be. And this caused bitterness for he felt if there is this much hate upon him he should be receiving more. There are others that he worked for that were receiving more but were not put in the spotlight as being hated. He was the one in the spotlight. So as I experienced this life, I was the – I was the spirit that experiences life in the physical manifestation, that was him. So I urged forward for him to open up his eyes, open up his heart, open up his crown to that which is Christ, which is God so that he*

may begin to see the light and understand what it feels like to not be bitter as you would say, not be upset, not be confused and to accept love, accept love into his heart, our heart, my heart.

Joe: Okay on another point, I'll have to double check the (New Testament) books that speak of Jesus, Yeshua's birth, but yours is the clearest. I, Joe Moris, in the 21st century – actually in the 20th century, raised Marisa and my son, Joshua on your account of the immaculate birth. Every Christmas we would read from Matthew on the birth of Jesus, of Yeshua. Question: who gave you the story? You have the – you have the most complete story of the birth of Christ as being born in Bethlehem. We understand it was in a stable because the town was filled with people because everybody had to register for the census, but who gave you the story of the birth of Christ, the virgin birth? Did Yeshua himself relay the story to you or did you find it out from other sources? Perhaps Mary, Yeshua's mother?

(Matthew) Not Yeshua. Mary Magdalene spoke of these stories over and over. Everybody spoke of these stories. I was able to take the information in which people spoke of and weed through the hearsay and weed through the things that I felt as if they did not belong because they would put a spin on them. For each person that told the story, it changed so much; just as we speak of things, the human mind will understand something different. For example, your misunderstanding that I went with Jesus because my brother told me to.

Joe: Oh, okay, sorry about that.

(Matthew) So things changed, things changed by the way that people hear them. I was able to have an innate

knowing inside of me that told me what was right and what was not right. So in essence, in essence, the higher self, my spirit, was communicating with me in order to bring this information forward. But I asked many people, I asked many people about this due to the fact that I was very skeptical. I wanted to understand, I wanted to know and know that I was on the right path doing the right thing. I gave up much and it was oh so worth it.

Joe: *When you were out on your ministry, when Yeshua was out on his somewhat, I think three-year ministry, there must have been huge crowds.*

(Matthew) Four years, two months.

Joe: *Four years and two months? There must have been huge crowds that just adored him and you listened to him teach and I was using the example in the 21st century, a rock-and-roll band becomes famous because they sing songs that everybody likes so they go out on concert tours and they travel from town to town and they sing the same songs over and over and over again because that's what the people know. Is that the way Yeshua was because you're very clear in your book on the various miracles and things that Yeshua had performed.*

(Matthew) No, each town was different. Each group of people was different just as this channel or, just as you would speak differently to different groups of people, this is what was shared. Some of it was more of a simplistic view of what he was explaining, some a little more complex. So, things were different, things were different indeed and I picked up on the lessons and recorded these lessons in which he spoke of. Yes, there are very similar things. You may look at it like a band has 10 songs and each town they go to they play 1 song. So if they go to 40

towns they're playing sometimes the same song 4 times or maybe even 1 song 10 times and the other songs 30 times separated between the other 9. So it just all depended on the conscious level of the people and this was his inner knowing and channeling in which he brought forward for we are all channels.

Marisa: Hold on. It feels like someone is literally knocking on my head. Somebody needs to give Matthew an antidepressant.

Joe: Come on Matthew, smile. Smile! When was the last time you were interviewed?

Marisa: He's irritating me because he's so like...boring. I mean he's so like not excited about anything, you know. I'm so used to talking to Eden and –all the exciting ones and he's just like, yeah, whatever. He reminds me of ......

Joe: Is he – is he upset that we're asking him these questions?

Marisa: Huh-uh. No he's not.

Joe: He's okay with it? I mean, ask him. Is he okay with this especially if he apparently seems bored?

Marisa: He's saying that he doesn't like to think of his life prior to the ministry.

Joe: Okay, then let's stay with the ministry.

[(Matthew) I will keep this short. I will keep this short and I will not try to teach a lesson within a lesson

within a lesson, but I must say, I must say that there are many different pieces of us. If this channel wanted to speak unto the 42-year-old that was Joseph Patrick Moris, she would see the 42-year-old, and that 42-year-old would come in as a holographic being or as an animated being, and she could speak unto him, because that is an energy, that is a time in this person's life that she is calling upon him. So at this time during this – as you call it – channeling session with us, she was speaking unto the tax collector. She was not speaking unto the apostle, the author. So many times you will hear the tone of voice change in a way in a sense that boredom, sadness, depression, anger, which was brought through to depict what my personality was like prior to my baptism, prior to my awakening but now the aspect of the "I" that is channeling through her at this moment is the proud one. I still stand tall holding the robes in which I wore, wearing the nobility clothes, as she describes it, that I wore, because this is the way that I would like to depict myself to you. This is not what I wore when traveling with Yeshua. But understand and know that there are many different pieces of all of us, and without getting too complicated, you can technically call us in at any age. You can call in the eight-year-old me and talk to the eight-year-old me. You could call in the 12-year-old me. And because there was no specifics truly placed on what age of that which was going to be spoken to, she happened to be communicating and channeling with the tax collector that was very unhappy with his life. But I, I still, I still am bringing in information now and must explain that I was not a bored person. I was not an angry person. For, the light of God filled me, surrounded me, enlightened my heart, brought love into my heart, brought love into my life, and helped me to beam the happiness that Yeshua brought into our lives. The contrast was insurmountable to anything you could ever possibly imagine, and this is why my soul chose this path in that particular incarnation to show contrast, to show the contrast of God. And I think this is what all of us experienced; it was the contrast. For each of us came from a different line of egotistical behavior and then turned into a lightened heart by the Holy Spirit, by God, by that which was the creator within, and we've shown that out to that which was the people, to teach them that they could do this as well. So I was not bored it was just the personality that unknowingly at the time, the two of you called in, which was the tax collector. I am very happy to be here and I love that the teachings in which I wanted to get out are able to make a glimpse into this book in which you are writing. I would very happily set forward and do my own book if you would like, but it would not be about me, it would not be about my life. It would be about the teachings of God, and the teachings in bringing them to people so that they can understand them today and depict the similarities between my teachings of that day, my writings of that day and what was truly brought forth into the book that you call the Bible.

Joe: *Yeah, but Matthew, you have got to know that theologians today are going to trash us because all the Christians look at that very last paragraph of Revelations where John said anybody who adds to or takes away from this book shall be basically doomed to hell.*

(Matthew) *Well, what I will say, my brother, is that we will never add to their Book. We will make our own. We are not adding to their Book and we are not by any means saying that their Book is wrong. Their Book is their book. We have said many things, many things* *through these channeling sessions that have not made it through this channel because she either does not resonate with it, does not understand it, or it is something that is much too big for her mind to understand. But see as time has gone on we could go back and do all of these same interviews and different things would come through for as the human progresses the words of God progress. So know and understand that these teachings will change but never, ever, ever the root of what I taught, never ever the root of what Paul taught, never ever, ever the root of what Luke taught, because we all had our own teachings and this is why, this is why the church chose to pull together the writings that they chose to pull together; because they were not all the same. They were different. There were other people who wrote things that were very similar, but ours were all a little bit different. But they did change them in a sense in that they wanted to make the words safe. They did not want to give too much power to the human mind. And this was God's doing. Do not think that this was Lucifer or the devil that came in and wanted to change God's words that we wrote in our journals, as you would call them, our scribes wrote. Understand that this was an understanding. You could not give a driver's license to a seven-year-old and expect them to be responsible. You can't expect them to not crash into things and kill people and kill themselves. They may be able to reach the pedals, they may be able to barely see over the wheel, and they may be able to turn that wheel but by giving them that much authority, that much power over something that is so powerful like a vehicle – and when I say a vehicle I speak of the human life, I speak of how a human life affects others – at that time on the earth plane, if people were given the amount of power and fully understood that – we have all talked about it – we do not believe that the world would be the same type of place. But this is why people are so excited about these times, because humans have finally reached, finally reached, the ability to responsibly drive the car.]*

Marisa: He says a lot of them aren't going to want to think about their life before the ministry because they felt as if they were reborn when they were with the ministry, if that makes sense. But – he says that everybody...he knows them and everybody will answer the questions, but he's saying – what is he saying? Hold on. Stop knocking on my head. Who is that?

Joe: Rosemary?

Marisa: Who is this woman?

Joe: Who is Rosemary? Let's ask Jesus. Jesus is going to know. Jesus, who's Rosemary? Why is she in this? We need your shield to be protecting us right now. We don't want any dark forces at all in this room. And anybody that isn't here with the Christ Consciousness needs to get out of here.

Marisa: She's a groupie.

Joe: She's just a groupie? She's a groupie –

Marisa: She knows so much more than anyone could tell you because she heard him speak.

Joe: Oh, she was a groupie of Jesus?

Marisa: Uh-huh...yes.

Joe: Okay. Well, we'll interview her. Tell her fine. I'll interview her then. In fact, let me finish with Matthew and I'll finish up with you for tonight –

(Matthew) Okay.

Joe: I want to know a little bit about when Yeshua was taken by the – by the military from the Mount of Olives. I think he was on the Mount of Olives or in the Garden of Gethsemane. I should check my bible.

You're probably upset that we've finished with Matthew just when we were asking about the crucifixion but don't worry, keep reading. You will also find Peter's and John's accounts in Book II are pretty comprehensive. I also mentioned that Marisa thought Matthew was boring but Matthew explained why he portrayed himself that way to us. He was a tough interview for sure. We've all been at parties or meetings where you ask a person a question and all you get is a dead-pan yes or no. It's hard to keep a conversation going with someone like that. Nevertheless, I found him intriguing. I learned much about who Matthew was.

Surely many of you wish I would have asked Matthew some very poignant and pointed questions about his book or epistle, but he already said that much was changed by scribes but that was how God intended it to happen over and above the misgivings of the authors. Nevertheless, I wanted to know the man, not the interpretation of his writings. I think that is what we have portrayed here.

Now, that silly Rosemary! Rosemary keeps popping in but according to Jesus it is okay. My guess is that she is going to have a completely different perspective on the Authors than even Jesus. Let's see how Matthew and Rosemary mix.

Chapter 3

Matthew And Who is Rosemary?

Recorded April 2014

I think you're just going to love this segment of the Matthew story. The more that is revealed, the closer we get to know those who brought us so much so long ago. Rosemary is a real character who had no part in the making of the Bible but she was loved by Jesus (Yeshua). Let's find out more about her relationship with Jesus and the New Testament authors.

> *Joe: What I wanted to know – when Jesus was arrested, what – what happened? What was inside Matthew's head when Jesus was arrested? In fact, let's back up for a second. At the last supper, according to our bible, did you understand what Yeshua was trying to say when he broke the bread and said, "Eateth this bread; this bread is my body."*
>
> *(Matthew) I heard him say it many times to many different people.*
>
> *Joe: Okay. So that wasn't the first time that had ever happened?*
>
> *(Matthew) No.*

Joe: So basically he had communion on a lot of cases, many times.

(Matthew) Yes

Joe: Okay. So he was teaching people about the (examples of) the bread and the wine....

(Matthew) And it wasn't necessarily a ritualistic thing that it has become today. It's become a ritual now. It's become a worshiping tool, and it was not necessarily like that at that time. It was a parable...in helping people understand that God or Christ is the loaf and when broken each one of us, each one of us is a bread crumb. Each one of us is a little piece of that loaf; and each loaf, each crumb is exactly the same as the loaf and has all the same aspects of it. So by people eating that it was the symbolism, the symbolism of showing them that each person has a piece of Christ in him.

Joe: And obviously the same with the blood being the wine...

(Matthew) Yes.

Joe: Did you have a feeling about Judas? Did you feel – were you surprised when you found out that Judas had – had fallen in with the soldiers and brought the soldiers up to take Yeshua away?

(Matthew) No. We all had an inner knowing that the ministry was going to end because we had this – we all had and were infused with the abilities in which your daughter carries, and we all knew that something was going to happen because it was the plan.

Joe: Why then – why then were there so few of you? There's no mention that you were anywhere near the cross when Jesus was put upon the cross. Our bible says that only Mother Mary and John were there. You were there?

(Matthew) We were there...I was there.

Joe: Were the soldiers at that time trying to round up all of the apostles?

(Matthew) No, not all, only those who put up a fight were sought after. I slipped into the background.

Joe: Yeah. That's the impression we get is that all of you slipped into the background. Then of course Peter –

(Matthew) John and Paul, which were not their true full names at that time were there (not the same as the Authors John and Paul)

Joe: Well, Paul the Apostle who wrote the Epistles for the New Testament had not yet met Yeshua.

Marisa: He was saying John and – trying to get the names. He's showing that's like who just said there's more – is it their names?

Joe: Yeah, they switched them. Jesus switched some of their names.

Marisa: Yeah. And he's trying to show me the names but they're written in a language that I don't understand with weird letters.

Joe: So Matthew, you slipped into the background then? You watched him die on the cross?

Marisa: I'm still trying to figure out those names. It's…. okay…..Matthew?

(Matthew) I could not watch. I turned my eyes in respect for a brother that I loved. He taught us so much and he always told us how much we taught him. This was something that no one had ever said to me, that I had taught him. For my life was about vengeance for my unhappiness that I brought upon myself, for I had siblings who were perfectly happy in their lives. I was in the background maybe 1200 feet away.

Joe: Oh, okay. So Jesus was off in the distance somewhat.

(Matthew) Everybody was circled around him.

[Marisa: He's saying that he did watch. He says that he turned his eyes, or he turned his head. He says that he actually did watch but he turned his eyes down in prayer, but that they all watched.]

Marisa: He's showing like dogs and everything, like scary-looking dogs. There's like two of them. That's weird. Did they all have dogs back then?

Joe: I don't know. So the soldiers had dogs with them? Or, the dogs were probably ready to eat the people who died because that was a form of punishment; I remember, it was a major form of punishment. That was the form of capital punishment, because a lot, a lot of people died on crosses. That was a normal thing.

Marisa: Oh, okay.

Joe: On the hill – what they called Golgotha, how did you feel when you knew that Jesus had finally died on the cross? How did you feel? Was it like the saddest day? Did it feel the same way as it was when your dad died or when your mother died or was it something different?

(Matthew) I watched him ascend.

Joe: You saw him ascend?

(Matthew) I watched him leave his body and go up into the sky.

Joe: How'd you see that? I mean –

(Matthew) I watched with my eyes. We had the ability to see these things. We had the ability to hear these things and sense these things. We were given these gifts that we had prior to being a part of this church, as you call it. But the ability to see, which I had as a seer, as I've been in past lives, we are each given these abilities so that people could see; that they can have those abilities too and still walk with Christ, walk with God. Because the Holy Spirit and the – as you would say now, the raising of the vibration, is what brought upon these abilities. So all the anger and the fear and the resentment that was removed from me when bringing the light into my field, my body, my heart and releasing these fears connected me to that inner source, the higher self that already knew

everything. It was going to happen. We were to share these gifts, which we did, with others.

Joe: So when Yeshua reappeared to you after his death, you weren't surprised?

(Matthew) No. I saw him, I saw him the same way as I saw him when he ascended.

Joe: In the Bible, our bible, the Apostle Thomas doubted Yeshua when he resurrected. It has been told that Thomas needed to put his fingers in the holes in the side of Yeshua before he was convinced it really was Jesus. Did this happen when you were there?

(Matthew) I don't know.

Joe: Did it happen? Maybe in the Bible – I mean I don't remember whose book in the Bible it is. I guess I'll have to double check which book's account.....there's some overlap between your book of Matthew and Mark's and John's and somewhat Luke's, but not all the books match up. But, it's pretty well known that Thomas, the Apostle was called the doubting Thomas because he wanted to really – he didn't even believe – oh, let me back up for a second. When he reappeared and was risen/resurrected from the grave...

(Matthew) His physical body was not risen from the grave. It was the energy body, the energy body. The physical body ascended, so it's no longer a physical body.

Joe: So I mean what you saw of him, was he like – when he came back, our understanding was he could pass through walls.

(Matthew) Yes, he was a spirit.

[(Matthew)   I must explain this. I must explain this to you. For just as I have said in the last entry that I shared with you, the words that come through sometimes come out a little bit differently based on the thoughts and the knowledge within one's channel's head. So what I was showing this channel as you were reading this is that I saw the spirit leave that which was the man and merge with that which was the Holy Spirit or Christ above him. I saw this and it appeared to be about what you would call 52 feet above his head. For I watched the light within him ascend which was his consciousness for that is all each of us are, we are just a ball of light. We are a ball of light with cells, with molecules, with atoms, spinning and evolving and carrying consciousness, carrying thought, carrying memories and these balls of light are what come and live inside an energy body that lives inside a physical body. For what happened, I will make this simple again, I will try to make this simple, I watched the consciousness that was my friend Yeshua leave and merge and become Christed. I watched the two energies merge together. When this happens sometime in the next three human days, the physical body will disappear because all bodies will come into line with each other; joining the physical and what you would say non-physical, they all come into line together. Therefore, together they all become spirit. Just as you see an airplane, it is physical, correct? But when it goes extremely fast it disappears. It does not mean that it has disappeared it just means that you cannot see it. So when we say that all the bodies merged together, it just

means that the cells were moving so fast because the spirit that was inside that body merged with Christ with such a high frequency that everything altogether disappeared to the human eye. That does not mean that it was gone it just means that it could not be seen.

Joe: *So when he was in the grave after the rock was rolled across the hole and he was locked away in the grave, and he was on a rock table, and he had a cloth over him, or whatever, he just flat dematerialized and blended with his spirit? He did not get up and --?*

(Matthew) *This could have happened on the cross. He could have disappeared, as we are calling it right now, on the cross. But this is not what happened. In fact, we will not go too deeply into all of the details because this will go slightly against what was in the books of the Bible, but the burial and the body and where it was and what happened is not exactly what is depicted in this Book. But for the beliefs, for the faith, for all of those who follow the Bible, even for us who were there, it is good enough. It is okay because confusion does not need to be brought into this situation. All one must know is that even if you just wanted to say that I was able to see a quote/unquote brother and physical friend die is okay but I watched the consciousness that sometimes suffered through a human lifetime; I watched that consciousness merge with the greatest part of him and I watched those two things come into line together and I knew that I wanted to be like that someday. That caused me to soften my heart even more. Yes, I missed the man. I missed his laughter. I missed the sparkle in his eye. But I knew that he was not gone for he was just not visible to the human eye. But he, God the divine, gave me the gift of being able to see the soul, as you would call it, the soul* *or the consciousness that was Yeshua, leave and merge with that which was his, as you call it, the higher self, or the Christed self.*

Joe: Wow!

(Matthew) Does that make sense?

Joe: Yeah it makes sense, but please answer this question if you can because (according to biblical accounts) you weren't there when Mary Magdalene went to pray for Jesus at his tomb on the third day. According to scripture, when Mary arrived at the grave of Jesus the big heavy stone that was rolled up in front of the hole to the cave was rolled away. So, to this day the Jews say that the Christians, or those who followed Jesus, went and stole the body and then made up this fake fable that he had dematerialized and risen. So even to this day, Jews don't believe Jesus was quote/unquote the Messiah because Christians had made up this story that he was resurrected, when in reality they went into the cave and stole the body and went and hid it somewhere. So my question is, why was the stone rolled away from the grave? Obviously it had to be rolled away so that Mary could walk in and see that Jesus was gone. Okay, I answered my own question.

(Matthew) No, that's not it.

Joe: What's the answer then?

(Matthew) The stone was already moved.

Joe: Who moved it?

(Matthew) The body had dematerialized and he had risen, as they called it, but there were those who wanted to catch a glimpse or see this Messiah, to see if this Messiah was really a man dead in a tomb. They rolled it aside, they looked and they saw that he was already gone.

Joe: Were these the guards? The Jewish guards? Or--?

(Matthew) It looks like three people, they look like Christians, they moved it, they opened it, he wasn't there. But they never said that they opened it and moved it. They said he did.

Joe: There were Jewish guards there. How did they get around the Jewish guards to roll the stone away?

Marisa: You know what? It may have been the Jewish guards. Were they the Jewish guards? He says, No, no, no. They weren't the Jewish guards.

Joe: I wonder what happened to the Jewish guards. How did the guys get past the Jewish guards?

Marisa: He says, men sleep.

Joe: Oh, okay. The guards were asleep. That's right. That's why they were persecuted by Herod or whoever.

Marisa: Who was persecuted?

Joe: The guards.

Marisa: Oh they were? He says --.

Joe: Yeah because the body was gone.

Marisa: The Jews were asleep. There were three people. They're holding fire. And they went and....here, Matthew's saying....

(Matthew) I would not call these Christians, per se, for what I would say would be (these three men were) disbelieving believers who wanted to see from curiosity and they had heard about this their entire lives.

Joe: Were they Agnostics?

(Matthew)   Yes, what you would say, an agnostic, they were seekers. They were people like you two. They wanted to go see for themselves; if he's in there, then he is just a man, he's mortal but if he's not there, then he's God. So, they moved this large stone, they rolled it out of the way. They opened the cave. Mary came in and saw he was gone but he had already been gone. So in order for him to dematerialize and rise, he did not need to move a rock. He did not need to open his tomb. He could have just gone 'poof' and not been in there. But in order for people to understand this, in order for people to see this, maybe there was some sort of divine intervention, but I do not know for sure. I will not say that for sure and set that in print for all of the times to read, all of those to read through the times. But I will say that if you feel as if it doesn't make sense because the Jews believe one thing [and] the Christians believe another, sometimes both sides are right. Sometimes they're both right, and they can both be right. And everybody can be right. It doesn't just have to be one way or another. But yes, humans moved it but it was not Jesus. Jesus dematerialized and re-materialized to show himself to those that he loved, those that he

trusted and continues to do it today. He will not materialize here in this living room but your daughter sees him on a regular basis. She sees him with her energy body eyes, and that is the body that we all appear in -- our energy body. And that energy body is what the soul lives in while the energy body is living within the human body. The human body just goes away and we keep our energy body.

(Matthew) Does that makes sense?

Joe: Yes, it makes sense. So, the three guys were just three agnostic guys --.

Marisa: He doesn't want to coin them as agnostic --.

Joe: Probably like teenagers? I'm going to picture them as like late teenagers.

Marisa: He's saying around 32 to 40ish. So they were older. They had grown up Jewish and became believing disbelievers. That's' what he wants to call them. He wants to call them "believing disbelievers". He doesn't want to call them agnostic because then that shows that there's a belief in God but they don't know what the god is. Instead, these men were "believing disbelievers" in Jesus. So, they believed in God, they knew who the one mighty God was; the I AM, and all of that. They knew the Old Testament and all of that for they believed. They just wanted to know if this Jesus/Yeshua was the Messiah so they just crept over there and they got in. It looks like there are three guys and they look like they are a little bit younger than me (36). It looks like there were more men with them but only three of them went over to the stone and when they got in the cave there was nothing there but they couldn't be like, "Hey, look, we broke in and there was nothing there." They just saw no one was there so they just kind of ran away. That's why Matthew says:

(Matthew) This may be more of Peter's thing, but we could sit here all day long and talk about the contradictions and the things in the Bible that either don't match or where two sides are both correct, and I think that's better explained by Peter. It's more in his category.

Joe: Matthew is deferring to Peter?

Marisa: Yes, and Peter's like, "That's me." But Matthew says:

(Matthew) I like to bring the feeling of what we talked through and teach people that it doesn't really matter about the specifics, but understanding and seeing the character changes in each and every one of us hardened men, and seeing what we are able to accomplish in such a short amount of time after meeting one man and learning his teachings, the changes we are able to make in a very harsh world should bring inspiration, wisdom and knowledge to those living in this world where it is much easier, much easier to have a civilized spiritual connection with God than it was back then. Because, it was thought then that God was not inside of you, rather God was outside of you. We learned that God was inside of each of us and that was my biggest teaching.

Marisa: He says, "I thank you," and he bowed.

End of edit from re-reading]

Joe: So when he appeared to you, he appeared to you, to your eyes? I mean, could you touch him like you're touching an arm or patting him on the back?

(Matthew) No.

Joe: You couldn't feel him?

(Matthew) No.

Joe: He was in spirit?

(Matthew) He's in spirit. My spirit could feel his spirit.

Joe: When he reappeared – I may have asked you this before – but when he reappeared to you as we call it "arisen from the grave," did it scare you or did you just expect it?

(Matthew) I didn't expect it nor did it scare me. When I saw him I was appreciative that I saw the brother that I had lost in the physical plane, but our beliefs in eternity and heaven were so strong, it was infused within us that many a times we often thought that we looked forward to going to the other side, as you call it.

Joe: A lot of people today feel that way too. I know I felt that way for a while some years ago.

Marisa: Yeah, me too!

Joe: So, after it was all over, after Yeshua had returned and reappeared to many, the Bible says that he was seen by over 500 people for forty days and then he just left....poof, he was gone. Did you have a sense of emptiness or did you have a sense of – of – of –

(Matthew) We had a sense of – of the job of carrying on the teachings he had given us. This was the only thing that we felt as if we needed to do which was to be carrying on with the teachings and to write out and to explain to those that were unable to hear his words, his ministries, explain to them in the best way that we could what he was teaching and where he was going with humanity.

Joe: Did you write your own epistle or did somebody else write it?

(Matthew) Somebody helped write it.

Joe: And was it written after Yeshua had gone home to heaven or did you do it on an ongoing basis during those four years?

(Matthew) After.

Joe: Completely after, but those....

(Matthew) Somebody else wrote some of the events down and taking those events that were written down and combining them with mine, I was able to write my portion.

Joe: When you went off on your own ministry, did you take another apostle with you? Did you, in other words, did you guys go out two by two like the Bible said that Jesus instructed you to do?

(Matthew) Yes but not with ones that you would know…but Paul also came with me.

[Editor's note: we don't know whether this was Paul his brother or Paul…Saul of Tarsus…Marisa doesn't want to guess and we didn't pursue this further. When we re-interview Paul of Tarsus we will ask him if he travelled with Matthew…].

Joe: Oh, okay, you went with other disciples of Jesus that are basically nameless…just other followers of Jesus then.

(Matthew) Yes.

Joe: Where did you go? Where did you go to minister? Did you stay right there or did you go to India? Did you go to Pakistan?

Marisa: Where's Bangladesh?

Joe: Bangladesh? Yeah, that's down there by India.

(Matthew) Bangladesh.

Joe: Wow. He went to Bangladesh? What happened? I mean, were you persecuted for your faith or did you die of old age?

(Matthew) I died of old age.

Joe: How old were you when you died, roughly?

(Matthew) 67.

Joe: Oh, you did live a pretty good life. Were you sick? Did you ever – did you die of a sickness or did you just quietly go to sleep one night and not wake up?

(Matthew) Dehydration.

Marisa: What's – he's showing me when your skin turns yellow – jaundice?

Joe: Oh, okay. So he's malnourished is what it was.

Marisa: Uh-huh.

Joe: Well, Matthew, is there anything else that you can – that you'd like to add to what I've asked? I know that I'll probably think of a hundred more questions for you as we start in with the others....

Marisa: He says, how can he think of any more questions than that? Ha ha ha ha.

Joe: You know, please smile for us here. Give us a break. Don't be so upset or what – are you upset that we brought you in here?

Marisa: He says no. He's just answering the questions.

Joe: Okay. Well, we're going to write a book and it's going to be about my interview with those of you who ended up with books in the New Testament. So after we write the initial drafts I'm going to be re-reading them again so you can add or subtract from these accounts. If I've made any mistakes you can add to it or what have you. This is the way we worked our first book as well. So Matthew, thank you very, very much. I really, really appreciate you coming in here.

Marisa: He has one more thing to say.

Joe: Oh, okay. That's what I was going to ask you. Do you have anything else –

Marisa: His higher self does, not him.

Joe: Okay. Yeah. Please, please, if there's something else you want to add, please add it right now.

Marisa: Okay. Here's his higher self. Let's kick the other Matthew to the curb and give him a beer and a shot of tequila and a little umbrella in his drink or something. He's still poking the fire. Ha ha ha ha. He needs a woman.

Joe: Ha ha ha ha

Marisa: His higher self says:

(Matthew's Higher Self) Dear Ones, this incarnation was spent, this incarnation was spent in a very serious soul, very serious soul. Do not take this as grumpiness or sadness or misery or anger. This is something that he needs to portray as the type of person that he is, for he is bringing this in. If he was to come in joyous and bubbly and happy, this would be a misrepresentation of who he was at that time. This does not mean that I am not joyous and bubbly, so to speak.

Joe: Oh, I understand.

(Matthew's Higher Self) So as you see the personification of who we are in the physical plane as opposed to the spiritual plane, you will see the difference and this is why the choice was given between the 5th dimensional self and the 6th dimensional self. You will see that when you are speaking with the human personification of us, you'll see that they are very similar to what they were like on the earth plane. This does not mean this is what he is like now, but he needs to come in and the others need to come in the way that they were on the earth plane at that time, otherwise it will not make sense. So please understand the information given and much of the information that was given is information that was partial, that was partial and not gone too much into depth, so when this is re-read there may be things added. There may be things added indeed, but understand this, understand that the incarnation in which I carry, in which I carry brought levelheadedness, levelheadedness and logic into religion and the skepticism, the skepticism that was carried was something that helped in that much questioning, much questioning took place and all these questions were answered.

And in addition to all of the questions and the information received, the visions, the visions in which I was able to give to the human aspect of myself were visions that were taken on by him and used in a rational way to write the things in which he wrote. Many of the books in which he wrote, five of them were excluded because they mentioned reincarnation. They mentioned the understanding that we knew that Jesus had lived before and will live again. Not just Jesus was born and he will come back. Also understand that we spoke of him as a brother, not as a god, so in speaking of that, the church took that out.

We also spoke of the relationships, the relationships in which we had together, in which we were brethren. We were brothers and sisters. We were a family as opposed to following and worshiping a man 24 hours a day, 7 days a week. He laughed and he kidded for he was a human being and he was inspired by the host in which was the Holy Spirit which was shared upon us and his higher self as well as Christ and God. And we understood this trinity and we understood the gifts in which we carried and we understood that we could too, just as he could, see the other side. Some of us heard, some of us smelled, some of us saw. We all had different gifts, and these were to be shared with the people of the world so that people would know even after his passing that they were and are still able to access these gifts that they were all born with without feeling guilty for them and not feeling like they were only worthy of gods; that only gods were able to do this. And the church, the church took out all of the abilities, most of them that we had that mimicked Jesus's abilities, as they call him.

Many of us could heal by touch. Many of us could do the things in which he did for we learned from him. He was trained extensively in India and other places far from home. He was trained extensively by Master Teachers in which were brought to him on how to raise his vibration, on how to heal, on how to breathe correctly, on how to meditate, on how to connect with, as you say, the higher self. And he taught these things to us.

We thank you, we thank you for taking these words and putting them into action for the information in which we have provided is to bring forth a personality of that in which I was, but the personality in which I was, was not a wonderful one [(prior to his baptism),] and this is what we have brought forward today. We bless you.

Joe: Thank you. Thank you, very much.

(Matthew) You're welcome.

Joe: We really appreciate it. I certainly appreciate it. Hopefully Marisa will remember a lot of this. Okay, well, we're going – we're going to interview – each time Marisa and I get together we'll be interviewing another one of the authors of the New Testament. So, Mark, if you're ready, we'll be coming to you next, but it's getting late right now, but let's go ahead and talk to Rosemary and get a little bit – a little bit from Rosemary if she's willing. Rosemary, are you still here?

(Rosemary) Oh, yeah.

Joe: Oh, my God. She must be important. Did Rosemary know Matthew? Or did we already ask that? I don't think they do. I don't think they know each other.

Marisa: Matthew seems like he joined in the ministry like way later on.

Joe: Oh, he was one of the last ones taken?

Marisa: Seems like it.

Joe: That's possible. Well, we'll ask –

(Rosemary) He was – he was –

Marisa: Rosemary is saying that the reason why his stories were so detailed is because there were so many people who had already seen everything so when Matthew came into the picture his emotions were not blinding what he was writing, since he hadn't experienced it firsthand.

(Rosemary) So he came in and he heard all the stories of all the people that were just so excited because they saw this and they saw that, that he just like wrote it all out emotionless.

Joe: Ah.... That's why he sounds so hardcore in the Book of Matthew.

Marisa: Oh, he does?

Joe: Very legalistic, yes. Very matter-of-fact, matter-of-fact, matter-of-fact.

Marisa: Yeah, he just – there's no emotion. She says – she says – let me see here. Why does she want me to stand up? Okay, fine. I'll stand up. Oooui, its 12:12. Make a wish.

Joe: Awwwww...the angels are here!

Marisa: If this was a book about something like Reiki I'd be a lot more excited. This is more bible stuff, so I'm kind of like, 'Eh, whatever." But I know that I'm going to learn stuff out of it, and I know that I like having Jesus in here. He tells cool stories. That guy was just fricking....bored me out of my mind, and he was boring.

Joe: His Higher Self explained why earlier. He is portraying himself the exact way he was at that time. So, now I'm picturing the way I'm going to write these accounts. I mean obviously you're the subject of all this; you're the person that's making this all happen.

Marisa: No, you are. I'm just channeling. So here's Rosemary. Rosemary, really, you want me to stand up?

Joe: Oh, please, Rosemary. Let Marisa sit down.

Marisa: Okay. She says – she says...

(Rosemary) It's about time!

Joe: Ha ha ha ha.

Marisa: She's going....

(Rosemary) Gosh. I had to listen to him the whole time!

Joe: So there are valley girls back then too, huh?

Marisa: She goes, "Oh, gosh. Thank you."

Joe: She's a valley girl?!!

Marisa: She's like jumping up and down, her arms flailing, and she says, "Huh, he was like a brother to me and Mary Magdalene, she was like a sister. It was like I knew them and they knew me, but they really didn't know me but I mean I – I – I knew them like – " oh, she's like so excited. She says....

(Rosemary) In this one time, this one time he was telling this story, he was telling this story about the salt of the earth and how the salt of the earth and the earth would just absorb all of the anger and sadness and madness that went on in the world because he said that just like, just like our spirit inside of us and just like the Holy Spirit, the Holy Ghost inside of us, the earth had a spirit that would just swallow up any anger and I would just lay

there. I would just lay there in the nature and allow this sadness to be taken away and it just changed my life, just changed my life.

Joe: *What was your sadness? Why were –*

(Rosemary) My sadness was the abuse that I was given up at 10 years old for sexual slavery.

Joe: *Oh, my God.*

(Rosemary) I was given up by my father, by my mother for money, and this was something that I was forced into, and this is something that I felt that demons were put upon me and I was told that. I was told that I would be nothing more, but when I joined this ministry and I joined it and began following it and feeling it, the energy of love that just protruded off of these people was enough to make me just feel the love, feel the joy and feel the peace. They did not even need to speak to me. For once, for once I spoke with Paul, I spoke with –

Marisa: *What is she talking about? A Randall or Ryan or something? That wasn't a name back then was it?*

Joe: *Not anybody that we know of.*

(Rosemary) The names that are in the Bible are very different, very different and there's a lot of things that happened that were not written down; and I know for a fact that some of the ladies wrote these things down because I knew them. I knew Mary. I knew her well. She knew me.

Joe: *Mother Mary?*

(Rosemary) No, and not Mary Magdalene.

Marisa: Not Mary Magdalene? There's another Mary?

Joe: Oh, there's a Martha and a Mary who were Lazarus' sisters.

Marisa: Okay.

Joe: Is she talking about Mary, Lazarus' sister?

Marisa: Yeah.

Joe: Oh, okay.

(Rosemary) I knew her very well, and she told me stories, and she let me know things that other people didn't know, and I am her cousin.

Marisa: Okay. She's showing me something like a family tree. Kind of like the daughter of a bastard child – that was related like she found – who's Lazarus?

Joe: Lazarus had died, had already been put into his grave inside a stone – like a cave, and Jesus came three days later and raised him from the dead.

Marisa: Oh, okay.

Joe: Was she there?

Marisa: Was he part of the – was he part of the ministry?

Joe: No. He was just a good buddy of Yeshua when they were growing up.

Marisa: Oh, okay. Yeah. She says that – she says that Mary told her all the stories and that she would – Mary was older than her and when she was young she would tell her stories of a god coming and someone who can forgive you of your sins and she was taken off (?)... then when she was 16, she escaped. She looks like she's about 23 or 24?

Joe: Who is this? Rosemary is 23?

Marisa: Yeah. She escaped and she killed the person that was attacking her. And she said that he was going to kill her. He had his hands around her throat and was – he had a knife and he was drinking alcohol, and there was a man that he was also with, like sexually with both of them so her and the man attacked the guy. And he wasn't royalty, but he was – he was wealthy and they took his coins and they escaped. But she and the man were not together by any means. He went one way, she went the other way. And she ran home even thinking they're going to come for her there. She was discouraged from staying there, but somewhere along the line she's saying she found Mary and she was brought to Yeshua to be healed and was forgiven and baptized. So she –

Joe: Did Yeshua – did she think of him as Yeshua or Jesus?

Marisa: She's calling him – she's calling him both.

Joe: Okay. Was she baptized by Jesus?

Marisa: Yes.

Joe: So this is something Jesus did? Jesus did do baptisms like John the Baptist did?

Marisa: Uh-huh.

Joe: Okay.

Marisa: She said she just had water put upon her forehead.

Joe: Oh.

Marisa: She was not dunked. It was a blessing is what she's calling it.

Joe: Oh. That's why the Catholic – didn't the – the Catholic faith just does the little cross on the forehead with Holy Water –

Marisa: Oh, really?

Joe: – yes, with holy water.

Marisa: Oh, okay, yeah.

Joe: And the Protestant religions do a full – full-immersion baptism.

Marisa: Yeah. She said that –

Joe: So Jesus did just the water on the forehead. That was probably how Peter started the Catholic Church.

Marisa: She says he baptized her and she actually felt the demons come off of her and he told her that the demons were not placed on there by God.

*(Rosemary) He told me the demons weren't placed on there by God, that they are placed on there by man; that there were demons around men and the only way to stay away from the demons was to trust in the Father and trust in the Father's love to surround, to surround us all. (*New Parable*) He compared us, he compared us to, as we have said, the salt of the earth, but he also compared us to a stone. He said, "Look at the stone. Look at the crystal, the crystal and the stone –*

Marisa: Hold on. She's showing me something. No it's not a crystal it's a....

(Rosemary) —a diamond." He compared us to a diamond and he said the coal is around the diamond and the spirit is inside, and when this coal can fall off then the diamond can show, but if we take the pressure and the love of the unconditional love that is carried within that of the Christ, we will then become christed one day and this love will just "poof" remove the coal.

Joe: To reveal the diamond....

(Rosemary) To reveal the diamond so that we feel like the diamond and we shine like the diamond and we are the diamond, and this is what I carried with me as I felt like the diamond. I released the coal and I released the demons, and this is something that I was forever grateful for and I will be forever grateful for and I will continue to teach his words and I will stay on the earth plane in this time, in this space to help the evolution of the planet, because people do not understand or put behind the teachings the excitement and the joy and the effervescent love that is expanding throughout the world. They put Jesus as God and he spoke his words of wisdom and he

*shared these words. He was funny. People laughed. People could not stop laughing around his presence (*a little exaggeration as Jesus mentions later*). He made jokes. He said these, as you say, parables, but he was constantly lighthearted. We sang and we danced. There are many religions that say that you cannot sing and dance. This is absolutely ludicrous. This is ridiculous, because we carry the childlike presence of fun and joy and excitement. And this is why I'm so excited to share this for as he (Matthew) spoke earlier, he spoke so seriously, because he came in later on and he heard the words and he heard the joy and he heard the excitement but had been so unhappy his entire life, so he translated (his accounts to you) through a very serious way. Although many things were lifted from him, this was a way that he brought these words in. And there is much joy and much excitement and much pleasure that was taken out of the words of the Bible and turned into such a serious book, turned into such a serious book that when one reads it they do not get joyful. They get joyful at hoping that they are good enough because they are reading it, that God will love them because God will judge them if they don't. There are so many more books that many of the ladies that I knew of wrote and they were not put in the Bible. They were not put in the Bible at all. I have watched over the years from here on this side as a teacher of Christ, of Christianity. I have watched how these things have been skewed and changed. I can tell you things that you probably wouldn't even believe because I have kept in tune with this religion.*

Marisa: *Eden, is Rosemary still for our highest and best good? Yeah?*

Joe: *Again, I don't –*

Marisa: Jesus, is she for our highest and best good?

(Jesus) Yes.

(Rosemary) I will bring excitement. I will bring joy. I will bring fun to the Bible. I will help people understand that it is a joyous thing as opposed to a very serious thing. I knew these people and I know them from this side. I do not ask that I be a part of this book or an interview of this book. I just want you two to understand that the energy that has gone into this book was done by man. And yes, they are factual. They are factual. The stories are factual, but there is much that can be added in the terms of energy and excitement and joy.

Joe: It's just that –

(Rosemary) Is this something that you understand?

Joe: Oh, I understand but it's time for us to cut off. You're – I don't mind, Rosemary, if you want to come back in after I interview – in fact, it's kind of nice. If you know all the disciples that we're going to be talking to, I would like to have your take on them after we speak with them – like after I interview Mark, I would like you to come in and give your – your – your take on Mark just like you've given us a take on Matthew. You were bored just listening to Matthew and you gave us a little bit of an insight on Matthew as well. One last question and then we'll see you next time. What about Jesus? Was he a pretty good-looking guy? I mean, was he a lady's man or was he just an everyday common-looking guy?

(Rosemary) Oh, he was very good-looking! He was very good-looking! He had light eyes which was not as common as in the men. They are almost angelic eyes.

Angels at the time were thought to be scary looking at times, but there were angels that people saw as being beautiful and these are the eyes in which he carried. They are almost out of this world. They changed colors. They changed colors when you looked at him. They did not change right in front of your eyes, but it seemed as if different days they may be grey, they may be blue, they may be green or aquamarine. His hair was light. His hair was light brown but sometimes it appeared darker. It was long just as those of you in these days see him as. It was long, but many times it was cut short. It was cut short during the summer times when it was very, very hot but it was grown out. Most of the time we all wore the robes in which you see us wearing and this is factual. But his face was always very young looking. He looked like a man but he was very young looking and this was something that the ladies absolutely loved, but they respected the fact that he was a holy man. They respected the fact that he did not frequent prostitutes and hang out with women that would do the things that a prostitute would do. He was not out looking for women, but women sought comfort in him almost like a father or an older brother that would protect them from anything. So yes, I would not say lady's man, so to speak, but I would say that he came across as someone that was strong, bold and noble and would protect them for there is nobody that he turned away in terms of healing and showing love. He did have – he did have two women by his side at all times and one of them he fancied.

Joe: Was that Mary?

(Rosemary) Yes.

Joe: He liked Mary Magdalene?

(Rosemary) Yes.

Joe: About how tall was he in comparison to Matthew, let's say.

Marisa: Five-ten.

Joe: Oh, okay. So he wasn't a real tall guy.

Marisa: He was Five-ten.

Joe: I used to be five-ten at that age...in my 30's.

Marisa: Five-ten; about – looks like 190 or something?

Joe: About the same as me. I bet he was strong. Did he have muscles from all his work on boats and ...

Marisa: Yeah.

Joe: Muscular guy?

Marisa: Muscular, but lean and – and sometimes he would starve himself or something?

Joe: Fast?

(Rosemary) And then his eyes would sink in a little bit so you could tell when he had gone into one of his mysterial fasts. He would fast for the people to release their energy because he would take on their energy when he would heal them.

Joe: Oh, and that was his way of getting rid of negative energy off of him?

(Rosemary) Yes.

Joe: Through a fast?

(Rosemary) Yes.

Joe: That's interesting.

(Rosemary) It's a cleanse. And I'm telling you this information from this side. I did not know all of this while I was there. I am telling you this from this side. In my excitement, I still have my higher self that is off doing what my higher self does, but I, the fragment, the Rosemary that lived at that time, I enjoy carrying on the ministry of Christ in the astral planes to those who are interested. I am a guide for very many people on the earth plane and I enjoy bringing Christianity with a fun spin into it to those of – those of the world that are opened to this side. I've channeled through with many different names. I've channeled through as Ellen, Elena, Elana. I've channeled through as (something) Humphreys.

Joe: Or are these the channels that you channel through?

Marisa: Oh, okay. These are the channels. Elena Humphreys, **(Schwarzkopf/Swartskov), a group in Germany.

(Rosemary) I like to work with channels so channels can bring through not just necessarily the truth. I – I like the emotion that's put behind it because there's – the Bible is void of religion.

Joe: The Bible is void of religion?

Marisa: Oh, oh, emotions – sorry.

Joe: Oh, emotions.

Marisa: She's – I'm reading a teleprompter now.

Joe: Oh, okay.

Marisa: Of emotion, yeah. It's void of emotion. It's – in the sense that – that – oh, just let her jump in...

Joe: There's no life – there's no life to it. It's like a matter of fact.

Marisa: Yeah, yeah. Here, I'll just channel again. I was telling her the teleprompter cuz she's like so excited. I'm like, "whoa." But she's saying there's no emotion put into the Bible and as you see that there's different parts of the Bible that if just a little personal story or a little bit about the – a child that was healed, not just the blind man was healed and God is great. It's – it's the story behind it or – or the child, the child that was sick.

Joe: Well, that's what is going to be in our book.

(Rosemary) And the disciples healed the child just as Jesus did and taught tons of people how to heal the people for he was not just a show-and-tell type of person; "Oh, look what I can do." He actually had schools of people and was teaching them how to do what he does.

Joe: Wow.

(Rosemary) *So these were things that he was saying; he would say... "Look, anyone can do this. Anyone can do this."*

Marisa: She's – she's – she's – hold on. She's talking about her mother or something like that.

Joe: Well, she's going to talk all night and –

Marisa: Yeah, she is.

Joe: – it's after 12:30.

Marisa: But she's saying basically she learned how to heal by touch. She could only heal mild colds and cuts and abrasions, but that she had gotten to the point where she could heal stuff.

Joe: Cool.

Marisa: But it's mostly emotions.

Joe: Okay. We're done, Rosemary. We're done with Matthew. Thank you for your input. You're very interesting, so I'm going to be – it's going to be fun listening to you after we do – after we meet with Mark.

Marisa: She says I'll be back if you want me to.

Joe: Okay. And –

Marisa: She's like a cheerleader.

Joe: Okay. And thanks to everybody. Thanks to everybody. Thanks Mom and Dad for being here. Thanks –

Marisa: Wait, hold on. Jesus just wants to say something really quick.

Joe: Okay. Thanks, Jesus. Thank you, very much.

Marisa: He's saying that – hold on.

(Jesus) The "thank you" must go to the souls in which you carry. The "thank you" must go to the drive in which you have for I just bring to you the story, the story of life, the story of creation and the story of love for as this channels through this channel, as this channels through into the words, into the pen, into the fingers in which type you will see, you will see that life will be brought to these words. Not everything that comes through will be things that are used, but everything that comes through are things that will teach you to understand that life was just the same as it is now back then. It was not something that was very dry just as the historians have made it sound. It was eventful and fun and exciting and there was tragedy, but tragedy was followed by victory and these things are brought through. There is so much depression that is circled around the story of my life, the story of my life, and what I want to do is help people to understand it was a joyous time and yet the people say, "The martyr, the martyr, he died for us, he died for us. Oh, we're so sad, we're so sad. We're so bad. He had to die for us because we're so evil." This is not the way that things should be portrayed in any way. They should be portrayed as; "He (Jesus), he worked so hard to learn how to heal people, and he raised his vibration, and you can do this too." And by being killed, this was a symbolism of what the human man, the human savage beast will do to those who are different than them, will do to those who rise above them in vibration,

because they are fearful of the things that they do not understand, just as the church is fearful of the things in which you two do. So if it was these times, if it was the Bible times, they would probably kill you two also – because they do not want to hear what you have to say.

Joe: Yipes....well, maybe there are some people today that would like us to shut up and go away.

(Jesus) This is exactly – you may not have been hung upside down on a cross, but this is something that you would probably be killed for, because anything out of the rhythm of what the church brings in, this is something that falls out of that pathway, out of the control and out of the jurisdiction of them. So please understand, my sister, please understand my brother, that we are partners in this. We are a team, and as soon as we can look at ourselves as a team and less as "Oh, mighty Lord, God, please give us this information and forgive us of all our sins," yes, this is true. This is what the Father does, but I am, I am a mouthpiece to this earth. I am an incarnation of this piece on earth to help people understand that we are all equal. We are all equal indeed, and we can all practice the miracles of life and healing. And one day, one day under my rule and under the rule of the Masters in which I work with and the Masters in which you work with, this world will be fully self-sufficient. Human beings will heal upon touch with each other. Nobody will be sick and old. It would be like the other planets in which we have touched upon in past sessions, for I have been here for each session prior to this, but this channel is unable to see me. Please understand that I have been giving a lot of the information in which you received in your (first) book (Answers: Heaven Speaks). You need to understand this, for each time you've called in the Christ Light, you called

me in. So see this and know this, that the information that has come through is very valid and it is time, it is time to see the recognition and yourselves that you are able to connect with these higher dimensions and this is good. We are proud, we are proud of both of you, and we are proud of the guides in which help you. We thank them and we thank you. We will protect you throughout this week until we meet again. We are very proud of you. Please remain grateful, happy, humble, yet proud because you are doing good things, and for this we are proud.

Marisa: That was your higher self that switched over at the end of Jesus's statement. It was like Jesus and then at the very end it was like your higher self jumped in. He's huge.

Joe: Oh, really.

Marisa: Yeah. Your higher self used to be like Eden's size.

Joe: This book's going to be fun.

Marisa: And now he's in the future.

Joe: This book's going to be really, really –

Marisa: If they're all like Matthew, I'll just learn how to –

Joe: No. They're all going to have different personalities.

Marisa: Okay.

Joe: You'll see. James – well, John – John and his brother –

Marisa: Don't tell me about them.

Joe: Oh, okay.

Marisa: Because I don't want to – I don't want to know anything about them before we….

Joe: Okay.

End of the recording

It always blows me away when Jesus comes in and speaks with us. I've told my girlfriend that I feel special that Jesus actually converses with us. She is basically a humble Mexican girl who grew up in a strict and legalistic Apostolic church in her little town of Guamuchil in the State of Sinaloa, Mexico. She says she talks to Jesus all the time and can hear him. I asked her "do you really hear Him"? She says she feels him and because He is with her she knows what she is supposed to do.

My girlfriend doesn't want me to use her name and is very nervous about me discussing our book with her parents. Her father's family goes way back to the 1500's in Mexico. Her family was instrumental in helping construct some of the Cathedrals that are in and around Culiacan as her ancestors were all preachers or priests. She made it clear that the Bible finds speaking to the "other side" as a grievous sin. I've tried to tell her that what we are doing is not evil. I told her that Jesus told us that what we are doing is not evil but her response is so similar to all those in the churches that I attend and that is "the devil is the great deceiver"!

I understand that Lucifer is devious, treacherous and bent on accumulating as many of God's childrens' souls as he can get away with but why in the world would Lucifer be glorifying Christ and the Son then? It doesn't make sense. I wouldn't be glorifying myself as evil so defending evil doesn't make sense in order to glorify God? Does it? Again, that makes no sense.

Marisa and I are doing what we are here to do. We are here to bring a personification to Christ. We are here to pass along and give life to Jesus and the New Testament Authors....and Rosemary? I like Rosemary and Jesus says its okay for her to be here and for her to give us her honest take on what she experienced.

The thing I most enjoy about Rosemary is her bubbly spirit. She just reminds me a lot of my pastor Rick's wife, Laurie. She is so bubbly and always looks happy. If you're down and out and Laurie comes by to talk to you then you almost instantly feel better. Her spirit is very bright and her light of Christ just exudes love and happiness. That is what we are receiving from Rosemary.

I especially liked when Rosemary spoke of how life was fun and joyous when with Jesus. She said he liked to keep people up with humor and good fun stories. (Jesus has since told us that he was serious about his sermons when he was teaching but that just like in any person's life, there is also down time and that is when He and all those around Him would partake in fun activities). I also liked that she described Him as well.

We now know that Jesus was about 5-10", was thin but muscular, had a young babyish face and had eyes that were out of this world. Jesus was a "rock star" and people flooded him just to touch him and be around him. I'm sure I would have been the same way. I would have loved to have met Him.

We Christians are always lamenting that we wish we could have witnessed Jesus as Christ. Well, this is the second best thing. Jesus is now talking through Marisa and I to all those who are curious and want to learn more about Him and his friends and co-workers.

And on that note, we move on to Mark.

Chapter 4

Interview with Mark

Mark was really tough to get a hold of. You'll find his type of personality to be like that you would expect from someone, anyone, from the Biblical times. It isn't because of the biblical times that Mark is the way he is though. Mark just comes across as such a foreboding soul; as a person which seems to run counter to the words of his Epistle. For Mark was not what I expected at all. I was under the impression that Mark was a somewhat young groupie that was real smart and wrote down everything he saw and then became buddies with all the other Apostles. It doesn't turn out that way at all.

Mark was once a member of either the Roman Army or of the Jewish Guards but he defected, he went AWOL. So, Mark spent his later life always looking over his shoulder. In fact, Mark was not able to go out and do ministry after the Resurrection of Jesus as much as the others because he was caught, tortured and killed.

Here is a quite lengthy session that teaches us a great deal. Mark is not the only one who is interviewed here. Jesus helped out a lot. Rosemary came in with more of a somber/instructional tone this time as opposed to the "bubbly" self we witnessed during Matthew's interview. The Higher Self of Mark had to come in to do a recap at one point and other higher spirits like Samuel, Daniel and St. Germaine also came in to help in this chapter. So, this is Mark.

<u>Recorded June of 2014</u>

Joseph: Okay. I'm hoping you're going to have pictured how Matthew looked. You pictured how Paul looked. You haven't described Jesus but I'm going to be asking all the authors to describe Jesus, just as we did with Rosemary. If Jesus is not in favor of the things that I ask, he can intercede and say, no move on. If he doesn't think we are going in the right direction and are not asking the right kind of questions then I would hope he would come in and say okay, go in a different direction.

(Jesus) Dear brother and sister, the aspect that you are channeling, the aspect that you are tapping into of each of these fellow men are aspects of that which is their physical existence. This was bringing the energy to explain how an understanding, the imagery or the way that the relationship showed itself on the Earth-plane (over two thousand years ago). Please note that when we call in these energies and we bring in these energies to this channel, there is only one to be brought in at a time or otherwise there is a chance that deception will come through.

Joseph: Good. I'm happy about that.

(Jesus) So when there is more than one (Apostle in here) there is conflict. For one may have another opinion about the other in this channel because tapping into the upper dimensional soul planes, this is something that far surpasses what most human beings can do. So, when tapping into these higher dimensions you are tapping into the soul so to speak; the aspects of the self that is evolved, but remember that the soul is the totality of every physical incarnation. So yes, only one at a time in one place so that this channel can handle them without interruption. I come in with the ability to lower my vibration not only to this channel but to every human

being on the planet as well for I am able to lower myself down to the human (energy level). This is how I reappeared to people (after the crucifixion) for I was in the spirit world, brought my density back and appeared to them and this is how I operated. For, I learned how to continue my learning as well as my teaching since then. I have grown very proud of the human race but, there is a need for a band aid so to speak, something to hold it together because there are those who are 'bleeding' to death and they do not feel as if there are any band aids to patch them up. For understanding that each one of us are a piece of Christ, each one of us are created by Christ and only through evolution of the soul, only through progressing through the levels so to speak will help that soul, that higher self, that spirit, to become Christed and then once again, to return back to home. This is what I have accomplished throughout eternity after I was Christed.

Marisa: I can't connect with Mark. That is why I was talking to Jesus.

Joseph: Is there somebody else Jesus can recommend that we talk to now instead of Mark then? If we go in order it is Matthew, Mark and then there was Luke. Luke was like the reporter. He was a doctor.

Marisa: Don't tell me anything about those that we are calling in…don't tell me about Mark, the one that wrote the books from the New Testament.

Joseph: He wrote his book, the book of Mark, the one that follows Matthew.

Marisa: Was he a scholar?

Joseph: I don't know. That is why we are going to interview him. I want to learn more about him.

Marisa: I just want to make sure we are interviewing the right guy. So I see a guy way, way, way off in the distance. He is way back there. He is walking this way. Jesus, has Mark's soul become christed?"

(Jesus) Yes.

Marisa: So is he in another world?

(Jesus) Yes.

Marisa: So can we talk to the human version of Mark? Can we talk to his hard drive that has all the stored memories from his Earth-plane existence?

{Marisa sometimes refers to the higher self as a hard drive because it is the totality of all of the lives that our individual spirit has lived over time}

(Jesus) Yes.

Marisa: Here he comes. He is coming closer now.

Joseph: Oh, good. (Long period of silence) He must have a reason for taking his time.

Marisa: He says he is travelling far.

Joseph: I'm excited about doing this book and I'm excited about these interviews. I'm going to be very excited when I can finally ask Jesus the question, lots of questions, but I don't even know what they are going to be yet. Let's just play it by ear. Right now I know we can interview him but I want him here just to be helping us and I'll have a one on one interview with him like we are having an interview with the different authors. Is Mark getting any closer?

Marisa: I'm asking him to show himself as who he was when he wrote these books.

Joseph: Or lived in the time of Jesus? It is possible that a lot of these books were actually written by friends of theirs or scribes and these authors would dictate to them.

(Marisa's higher self and Abraham) These were stories that they told that were passed on. Many of the stories got skewed. Many of the stories were up for interpretation. Imagine this, sitting around a fire and somebody is telling a story. Each of the 12 people sitting around the fire all hear this just a little bit differently and then go off and they tell someone, who tells someone, who tells someone. At this point the story has been changed, not by mal-intent but by just an understanding that it is different than what the first person who spoke the story was attempting to create. Many of the books are these stories but were circumvented by the church to appeal to the masses and that which brought the people to their knees in pledging their faith and love to the church rather than to God.

Marisa: So Mark is that you?

Joseph: Who was that talking?

Marisa: That was my higher self, but my higher self was talking to Abraham and Jesus

Joseph: Not every Apostle wrote a book. Well they all did, they all wrote letters and things but (the Roman Emperor) Constantine created the church and the New Testament by taking all of the letters from all of the different Apostles and other people who knew Jesus. In our last session you said that they had 222 Epistles and they chose 27. There are 27 books in the New Testament.

Marisa: And I knew that?

Joseph: Yes, you said they had 222 so a lot of those Epistles would have been by the Apostles of Jesus but for whatever reason Constantine didn't use those and he used 13 of Paul's. So, we'll be interviewing Paul again.

Marisa: Paul is the cripple right with the weird hand and the little teeth, weird teeth?

Joseph: Yeah.

Marisa: Mark, are you an ascended master now?

(Mark) Yes.

Marisa: Are you an ascended master that has chosen to stay around the Earth-plane?

(Mark) No.

Marisa: Did you create the universe that you are in and now watching over?

(Mark) No. God creates everything. God has a hand in creation no matter what we do. The clinical worthiness of one's soul begins to be defined by the light of God, and that soul begins to have the knowledge and the ability to

do what God does, especially when one reaches Christhood (accomplished after leaving the human existence). You may go to (heaven) and create anything you would like. You may stay here and help others just as Jesus has done. I have chosen to live an existence on one of the planets in the Pleiades system which is a fifth dimensional aspect of me.

Marisa: Can I call you in closer if I get the fourth dimensional aspect of you? Jesus, since he is on another planet, if you can help me connect with him that would be great. It is like I am Skyping him. This is weird. I've never seen someone so far away. Jesus, are we okay with interviewing him?

(Jesus) Yes dear child. You may do what you please for I allow all of this in the curiosity that carries with that which is the both of you which is what ignites the desire to love and to be loved in those around you.

Joseph: Well, there are some questions I would like to ask Mark from that same vein. I initially learned most of what I know about Mark from the Urantia book. They described Mark as what we would describe as like a groupie today. He was always kind of on the fringes being that he was so enthralled with Jesus. So he would follow Jesus everywhere and he would listen to him speak.

Joseph: Well then let me ask this question and maybe he can answer it or maybe not. At the last supper Jesus retreated to an upper room with the Disciples, with the Apostles. In the Urantia book it says that it was Mark's parent's house where Jesus took his last supper before he was crucified. Is that true Mark?

Marisa: You said it was whose parents?

Joseph: Mark's. According to the Urantia book Mark was younger than all of the Apostles and he was...

(Abraham) Mark lived in a home that was not a parent's in which he was raised by for they were long gone.

Marisa: Let me just talk to Mark by myself. Much easier, okay, I've never had such a hard time connecting with someone.

Joseph: Should I pose a question or have I already?

Marisa: The question is about the house.

Joseph: Yeah, was the house of Mark's parents, the location where Jesus had his last supper.

(Mark) Where we grew up was incongruent with where we lived when we were "grown up." From the time that we were 16 or 17 we were moving from place to place whereby there were hosts so to speak that allowed for us to stay in their home for a small fee.

Marisa (and Mark): Were these your parents? **No.** *Were your parents alive?* **No.** *He is making it sound like a foster parent or something like that, like someone that took him in. It was like his dad's brother and wife. Was it the brother and wife?* **No.** *Okay, so was it the sister and husband?* **Yes.**

Joseph: His sister and his sister's husband let him grow up with them?

Marisa: No he was living with them from the time he was 17. He already felt that he was grown up.

Joseph: Where was he living until he was 17?

Marisa: A cottage outside the city living alone so to speak.

Joseph: What city?

Marisa: The city of Carol. He is spelling it, C A R like Carol, but there are little weird lines above the letters.

Joseph: Oh my gosh....he must be writing it in Hebrew.

Marisa: That's the problem on account he is speaking it in a different language. That's what I just came to the realization of. It is like when people come in to see me and we basically call in like grandma and she only speaks Spanish or something like that.

Joseph: Well I certainly can't speak Hebrew. So I think we still have to communicate with his higher self.

(Mark) Art now haveth that which is seeded from the fruit of life for the poetry and the visions in which I write are something that would help each on their flight to the higher realms of consciousness for when the words are written, when the words are displayed, each person who reads them will read something different indeed for what I write is like a spade within the deck in which you play. Is this about a controversial one?

Joseph: Well, according to the Urantia book, Mark's books were read, his letters, his Epistles, books...there *were five of them that made up the book of Mark but one of the five was lost or deleted or burned.*

Marisa: I think there were seven.

Joseph: There were seven?

Marisa: Yeah.

Joseph: One or two or three were lost or they were basically copied. According to theologians, Matthew and Luke basically copied from Mark's writings.

Marisa: Okay, well basically he is saying that the stuff that he wrote was out of the ordinary because he had the visit. Most people that wrote the Bible and the people that followed Jesus felt the Holy Spirit inside of them and they would feel that urge to accept the life of Christ basically into their heart and it raised their (using your language) vibration.

(Mark's Higher Self) Mark the human had the ability to connect with, as you call it, the "other side". For his lifetime, for when he was young, he took care of himself when the parents were gone for they did not come back.

Marisa: Living in a home outside the city of Carol? I can't read that. Is that like Bethlehem or something like that?

Joseph: Are you asking me?

Marisa: No, I'm asking them. They are spelling it Carol. It is their letters I don't understand. There are like little lines and dots over them. Oh, is it backward? Lorac? No. He wants us to look it up.

Joseph: We could look on an ancient map or something.

Marisa: Yeah, so he...

(Mark) What we did was from birth, we knew we were different and writing the findings from the other side I learned to write by one that I trusted, but not everybody could write.

Marisa: Is that true?

Joseph: Yes, they weren't all educated to write. So there were scribes that could be hired or there were scribes that followed Jesus. So when Jesus was gone the scribes would go with the Apostles. When they went out to their ministry almost all of the books that were written were written by somebody else in the author's name.

Marisa: He is saying he wrote seven books. If you say the first book is 4 pages it was really 11. If the second book is 2 pages it was really 12. If the third was 7 pages it was really 20. So things were kind of out of sync, changed.

Joseph: By Constantine, by the church?

Marisa: By the church and by those who rewrote his story.

Joseph: They rewrote his story? Does he agree with the story though as it is now in the Bible? I mean does he bless what is there that we as Christians read?

(Mark) Absolutely. It rings true in love and guidance and wisdom of that which was one who existed at that

time and existed and shared the light of Christ through the man that was Yeshua. We bless anything, or any document, that looks highly upon this time (of Yeshua), this incarnation in any of our lives whereby the point, the point of these books that I wrote, were out of retribution to the government....retribution to the government and their inability to see how the common man lived and these wise men, as you would call them, guides came in and they shared with me the many writings in which I had help with to free souls and helped them to believe that in which they could not see. I bring true the essence of loneliness within the writings in which I wrote because I always felt so alone until I felt as if I had joined forces with the group. In joining the ministry I felt it more as a collective as opposed to each being individual.

Marisa: He showed me like green grass and like apple trees.

Joseph: The group that he joined, was that with the Apostles or did he feel lonely because he was being left out? Again, Mark was not an Apostle.

Marisa: No, he wasn't being left out. Let me see here. Were you being left out?

(Mark) No, but never having a family to truly connect with and seeing others that did, and seeing that their parents were everything, and knowing that mine left and didn't come back...my father left and did not come back, whereby my mother took care of us. There were 6 of us and she died in childbirth (with the sixth child). The oldest was 6 years older than me.

Marisa: He is calling him Jacob.

Joseph: His older brother was Jacob?

Marisa: This is not the Jacob that you are thinking of, but his name was Jacob.

Joseph: Yeah, there was a Jacob in the Old Testament.

Marisa: Okay. His mom was a God-fearing woman and she believed in like multiple Gods. She would pray to different Gods for different things and he always knew deep inside that there is something different and he chose to investigate that.

Joseph: Something different about what?

Marisa: Something different about worship in God and creation.

Joseph: How old was he when he realized that?

Marisa: About 14.

Joseph: About that age 13, 14 are when Jews are supposed to go into school to learn the Torah and the books of the prophets. Did he go to a Jewish school?

Marisa: He said he did go to a Jewish school. He went to a Jewish school for only one year but his mom died and he quit school and had to go to work.

Joseph: Okay, most or all kids did that too.

Marisa: Did he go into some sort of battle or something like that with horses and shields and swords?

Joseph: I don't know. That is what we are trying to find out; what kind of person Mark was; what his experiences were through life. How old was he when he met Yeshua, Yeshua Ben Joseph?

Marisa: He is saying 29.

Joseph: Really. Wow. How did they meet or did they ever meet? Did Mark ever talk to Jesus directly?

(Mark) Yes, very briefly at different times. I looked at him as an inspiration but not as God. I looked at him as an example to live by and then, when beginning to understand the ministry, (I) began to understand the divinity inside each of us, with God-like abilities to create the life that we want...or (have it) just at our fingertips. Yeshua showed us how to access these just as he did, and this is when I began to see the council, or as you keep calling them, three wise men, and they would come in and tell me stories. I would tell these stories to others and they would agree that they were correct (even though) I was not truly there. I was looked at as a form of a seer that would see things, especially when I dreamed at night. I was a bit mystical and different than the others and I felt very different, but I owed the ability to have a higher learning, having a higher reason to Yeshua; for he took many complicated aspects of spirituality as you call it and made them simple. The most important thing to understand in spirituality is keeping it simple. There are so many layers of existence, so many travels that the soul will do and take just as I am (taking) at this time. So keeping things simple in an understanding that most people only understand simple but still bringing through the virtue and the love of Jesus was important. The government, which is much like the church, was something that I rebelled against. There were many who

rebelled against the government for they were taking people down that did not live by their standards. After reaching adulthood I was mentored by someone that would be called a scientist today, taken under his wing and taught the Scientology of the mind.

Marisa: What is Scientology?

Joseph: That's a modern religion.

Marisa: He's using some words; remember he is not speaking English. I have to translate it.

Joseph: Through his higher self?

Marisa: Yeah, but it is funny because I'm hearing him talking in a different language. It is almost like the voice-over thing. It is kind of frustrating. I actually feel like my chest is going to explode.

Joseph: Well take a breath and relax. I wonder why it is so difficult. I've had a completely different idea of who Mark is or was. When he first met Jesus, Yeshua Ben Joseph, what was his opinion? You said earlier you didn't think he was God but you thought he was a wise man.

(Mark) I'll give you an example as to show how to in a simple way praise the Lord and bring the Lord within us for upon meeting Yeshua or Jesus as you call him, my life completely changed. I shed the bitterness and the anger and the sadness, the retribution, the disgust for human beings, and fell into line with exactly what the Christ was speaking through Jesus.

Marisa: Rosemary is like, "Can I talk?"

Joseph: No, not yet. Well I want to get her take on Mark because she is certainly going to know Mark.

Marisa: He is a lot younger than the people so he was kind of like a lost soul. This is his higher self. ..He is kind of like a lost soul (who is) just kind of roaming around looking for someone to love him and when that happened he felt renewed. It is kind of like when people are so into a celebrity that they like to think that they know them. He is saying that he had contacts with them and that he travelled to seven cities.

Joseph: I dare not ask what cities because I don't understand Hebrew.

Marisa: Yeah. He travelled to seven cities and Jesus was usually staying at each place for about a month; one moon cycle.

Joseph: Rosemary mentioned after the Matthew interview that Jesus wasn't portrayed accurately because he (actually) had a good sense of humor and he liked laughter and he kept people happy and laughing. Is that something that Mark saw? He was not in the inner circle of Jesus and the Apostles but rather he stood afar or was a part of a larger group that followed Jesus around. Was Jesus a light-hearted happy person?

(Mark) Absolutely! He was joyous and happy. He was serious when he needed to be but that was just in congruence with someone who felt they were unworthy. He would explain to them that the forgiveness of self is the key to existence for when one forgives oneself they are able to be free. There are many things in many ways that those on the Earth-plane witnessed; the rules that

were lived by, the abuse of power, the hate, and the human emotions that come along with this existence.

Marisa: Hold on, did you hear that noise?

Joseph: Maybe it was my stomach.

Marisa: No, everything just got muted. It was here. He is just getting closer. Now he is right up in my face.

Joseph: Did he see... I know I'm bouncing around and we'll figure it all out upon how we're going to put it all together in the book, but did he experience the resurrection of Jesus?

Marisa: No.

Joseph: So he didn't get to see the resurrected Christ?

Marisa: No.

Joseph: He wrote about the resurrected Christ in his books. Are these things that he learned from others?

Marisa: Other stories were told. Stories were told and he was 14 days away from where they were, 14 hours away. Wait, 14 hours or 14 days? 14 hours away. 14 hours? Speak English please. Okay, hold on, higher self, can you please open me with the ability to translate what he is saying. I want to connect to the highest aspect of him.

(Mark's Higher Self) He still understands the individuality of who he was. Whereby thus may you ask; why would I be in this dream to understand who as you say Jesus was?

(Mark) I was looking for a home. I was looking for people. I was looking for someone that cared for me and the people in which following him truly cared and admonished that which were hate, jealousy, and greed. Having just one taste of this and the feeling of belonging, I never wanted to leave. Many stories were told and I felt to keep the memory alive somebody must write down and keep record of what had happened. For example, four days prior to the legendary crucifixion, Jesus' left leg was broken.

Joseph: What? Who broke his leg? How did he break his leg?

Marisa: It was either his leg or his ankle. He is showing his ankle. It looks like a soldier or something like that.

(Mark) So he was prepared and ready and knew what was coming but he showed no fear, for every human being is expected to not have fear but the human ego, that which makes us human while on that plane, fear is derived from the mind in each human being. He taught how to not have that fear by teaching and understanding that this is only temporary here. It was that lesson about fear that I adored and which I expressed through the understanding, which I got in the writings in which I "wrote." The first two (books) were written by me... the professionals...

Joseph: Were probably dictated to scribes?

Marisa: Yeah, they are showing him talking and someone else writing it. Like they are sitting on the floor or something like, kind of like how I sit on the floor and just writing. He wasn't very... It looks like his sister was kind of wealthy. The house looked like it was like a two-story.

Joseph: Did Jesus and the Apostles stay at that house when they were in town? Of course they had to stay somewhere when they stayed somewhere for 30 days in each city that they went to.

Marisa: They stayed in different places. He did not follow them to all the places in which they went.

(Mark) I felt a responsibility to take care of the family in which I had.

Joseph: What kind of family did he have?

Marisa: Sister and all of the kids.

Joseph: Did he ever marry? He never married and had children?

Marisa: Let's see. He married at 22 and it looks like just like his mom, the lady died in childbirth, the wife.

Joseph: His wife died in childbirth?

Marisa: It looks like it, yeah, and the kid too.

Joseph: Oh no. No wonder he felt so lonely.

Marisa: Yeah and that was at only 22 years old.

Joseph: Wow. What kind of jobs did he do to make money to buy food before he met Jesus and followed Jesus?

Marisa: They keep showing like a...they keep showing something like a dryer, he is showing like a hole with a hot like... it could be a smelt, like a mason or something.

Joseph: Okay, you are probably right. He was probably just a regular laborer. I'm not sure what they... I mean they certainly minted... I mean the government minted coins and things like that that are made...maybe (he was) a glass blower or something?

Marisa: He is showing it's almost like weapons or something like that, like swords or something.

Joseph: He had a job making swords?

Marisa: Yeah, it is like specialized in doing stuff like that and odd jobs here and there, but again he never felt like he belonged anywhere.

Joseph: And he did not experience the resurrection? Did he truly believe that Jesus had resurrected?

(Mark) Yes and when I state that I do not believe that he was God I only state that the understanding that I received from the wise men as we have been calling them, not to do with speaking with the wise men from prior, but understand that what they explained to me (was) that everybody is God inside and everybody has these abilities. It was much easier for me to understand for I saw things that others did not see. I knew what was going to happen before it happened. I saw the aftermath of the hanging, the crucifixion. I saw the aftermath and I saw the sadness in the ministry, the group. It had been so lively, upbeat and happy. Yes, there was much disturbance within the group because of the slander that

others attached to them, but this did not penetrate the shield on which they carried. This was admirable.

Joseph: He speaks as if he is a part but he is also.... he is a part of (the group) but he is also apart from. He is from afar in other words... Did the Apostles take him in as a friend or was he with a group of people other than the Apostles that he knew?

Marisa: He looks like he bonded more with them after Jesus. Didn't they all get killed with him (Jesus)?

Joseph: No. That is why we are going to find out where everybody went. How did he die and how old was he when he died?

Marisa: I think 43, yeah.

Joseph: And how old was he when Jesus... Well he must have been pretty close to Jesus' age if he met him at age of 29. Did he continue on? Did he become a minister? Did he go out and preach the gospel of Jesus.

(Mark) I began to extrapolate the words of the wise government, and

Marisa: He said that kind of sarcastically.

Joseph: He did what? He took on the whole...

(Mark) I extrapolated the words and the stories that were being told to people about Jesus and put truth into them for I knew it was going to happen. The wise men told me it was going to happen and people put blame upon him for being a bad person. My goal to resurrect him so to speak in form of character is what helps the

group of people, of 32 people that surrounded him at all times to accept me. There were three in particular that became like family to me.

Joseph: Here is my question then: What did they do, did they take all of the stuff that you wrote or did you give it to the government or the church? (Long silence)...He is not saying anything? At that time, Rome was oppressive although there weren't any real wars going on. The Jewish hierarchy, the priests of the Jewish faith were kind of mean also, and they had their own laws and their own judges. So those people, my guess, those poor people were walking on eggshells all the time if they were going to be judged by the Romans or were going to be judged by their own church of the Jewish faith, the Jewish church.

(Mark) But we didn't care.

Joseph: You didn't care about what?

(Mark) The judgment of others, for it was just so much pride that came with knowing the truth. I look back now at the darkness, the darkness of which I was living in.

Marisa: It looks like he was like a hound or something, or something about his chest because my chest feels like it is going to explode.

Joseph: Was he a martyr for Christ? Did he die because of his faith in Jesus?

Marisa: No. (Mark was killed by being dragged by horses). He keeps showing me some sort of like battle with like horses but I'm going to look up here a little bit. He is very hard to talk to. I've never had such a hard time channeling someone before, ever. He is very hard to connect with. There would probably be an easier way to connect with him than this.

(Marisa gets up and walks away and Mark follows)

Joseph: Don't go away Mark. Don't go away.

Marisa: He is still here and following me.

Joseph: Oh, okay. (A long silence while Marisa is away.)

Marisa: Let me take a bite of this candy or something. This energy is knocking me out. Let me stay awake here. I'll stand up for a second. Okay Michael, can you reseal the room? Okay, so he says recap.

Joseph: Mark wants us to recap?

Marisa: No, he is giving a recap.

Joseph: Okay.

Marisa: He says the questions are spacing things out too much.

Joseph: Yeah, I'm random all over the place. Yeah let's have his recap.

Marisa: Okay.

(Mark) (Alone? unintelligible) at 7, father was a...like a hunter, he never came back, mom died, (I) grew up alone, very alone.

The Bible Speaks   Book I   Featuring Matthew and Mark

Marisa: He was married and lost his wife, he is left-handed, schooled, learned to write, wanted to be a scholar but left school to fight like a fighter or something, a sort of warrior. Were there wars back then?

Joseph: No, did he join the Romans, the Roman Army?

Marisa: It looks like the metal like chest plate things with the horses and the swords.

Joseph: He probably became a soldier, a Roman soldier.

Marisa: (He was a soldier but not Roman. We understand Mark was actually born in Egypt and eventually ended up in Jerusalem but before fleeing to Jerusalem...he was more like a cop). He was taught how to be like a swordsmith where he created the weapons but the government was so corrupt sending them into battle to die just to show people that they fought for what was right when really it didn't, and they would hurt innocent people.

Joseph: Him too? Mark also?

Marisa: He wasn't hurt. He saw many things happen.

Joseph: But did he ever hurt people?

Marisa: Yes.

Joseph: Enemies?

(Mark) They were told they were their enemies but these were innocent people that had different beliefs, different ideals of what the government should be. The government believed in different Gods and different idol

worship, but many proclaimed to have one God. These were wars over religion so-to-speak, wars over beliefs and there was ten of us who revolted and left. So I basically went undercover and hid within the people.

Joseph: *You went AWOL then...*

(Mark) *I hid and in the city met Jesus. There was so much criticism and so much anger toward the group of people in which surrounded him by so many people because they (were) fearful of the messages that he was giving. They (the messages) were against the government and against the beliefs that were already set in place. So I had to be careful but at the same time there was something about the group and about Jesus that kept them safe. It was like an invisible force surrounding them so I felt safe. Eventually I was caught and killed.*

Joseph: *Oh. Was this... This had to have been after the crucifixion that he was caught and killed.*

Marisa: *Yes, about 15 or 18 years later. 15 years later? 15 to 18 years later is what they were saying. The years were different back then.*

Joseph: *Well if he was like in his early 40s then....I'll have to figure out that timeline again. It sounds like he was about Jesus' age, but if he was killed about 18 years later he would have been closer to his 50s than his early 40s.*

Marisa: *No, he met Jesus at 29, followed him and the crucifixion was when he was 32, right Mark? He said there is such a difference in the years that we have now than the way they judged time then. They went by the moon cycles.*

Joseph: Oh, okay.

(Mark) There were days added here and there and sometimes there were 13 what we would call months in a year.

Joseph: They went by the moon, yeah.

(Mark) So when you go by years it is a lot harder to translate into this time. So this is why I say 15 to 18.

Joseph: If it was many years after Jesus died that you were caught and killed, as I'm guessing you were a deserter from the army, what did you do? Did you stay with the group? Did you go off on your own?

(Mark) I pretty much followed them. I stayed in different places. Paid a coin or two to stay in homes where I was not noticed. They knew I would follow. They knew I would be there, but I wasn't really a part of (the formal group of apostles) for there was too much focus on them. Everybody knew who was in that group so to speak, the 32.

Joseph: The 32 did not include the Apostles?

(Mark) Yeah that did.

Joseph: Oh, so he was in a group of 32 and of the 32 were the 12 Apostles as well.

Marisa: Yeah. Actually there were 13 Apostles, 14, a female.

Joseph: There were only 2 female Apostles?

Marisa: Yeah, was it the Apostles...

(Mark) The ones chosen by Jesus to be his messengers...to carry his word, they were the closest to him. They protected him, they would sleep close to him, they fed him, and they found places to stay and acted as security guards when there were crowds. They were the administration with Jesus.

Joe: Mark was not one of them, but his was the second book in the Bible...

Marisa: So he says, but he must be a part of it if he wrote a Bible book.

Joseph: Yeah, I mean that is the truth. The Bible names all of the Apostles and Mark was not one of them. So theologians are kind of (unintelligible) ____. That is what our book is going to be about. Our book, like Jesus says, we're going to sew-up holes. Nobody knows these guys or why Mark's writings became the second book right after Matthew in the New Testament. So his writings were, you know, phenomenal. I mean at least to the church some 300 years later. They used his letters to write the book of Mark, or to include the book of Mark. But Mark has now said that he actually had seven books or seven...

Marisa: Uh huh.

Joseph: Were those seven books combined into the one book or was one of the seven used by Constantine?

(Mark) It was rewritten as a combination of them.

Joseph: The church actually took their letters and rewrote the letters?

(Mark) Yes.

Joseph: Oh no. How am I going to deal with that? Is Jesus still here?

Marisa: Yeah.

Joseph: Jesus, you said you will shut this down if I go negative or if I tried to change…. He's detracted from the Bible and could persuade people not to trust the Bible.

(Jesus) Many things are changed but with the guidance of God over those who rewrote the book or condensed the book. One may believe that those who wrote the book or rewrote the book were putting in that which was only positive so that people would agree with and worship me as Christ for there were many things written in many of the books that carried a negative connotation toward that which is the one true God. This is not to say that Mark said anything negative but in the churches eyes this was. So what better than to take all of the positive aspects of his writing and put them into a condensed version of what he wrote? So you do not need to speak of the fact that the Bible is wrong. You may say that man put this information into books to make it more understandable for the people at the time. But there must be an understanding that there are holes and there are more. There was more written. This is not saying that the Bible is wrong. This is saying that information is missing and this is okay to express. For everybody, even the most devout Christians as you call them, have doubts about why there are holes in the stories in the Bible. The Bible

is really just a book of faith, a book of understanding, and that which God is, and I was the messenger. The book was inspired by God and brought to the people to bring faith.

Marisa: Is this still Jesus? Yes. Abraham and Eden are still here. Yeah there they are. Okay, Rosemary. This candy is helping me to stay awake. Their energy is so strong.

Joseph: Well thank goodness Jesus came in and gave us a better explanation.

Marisa: Uh huh.

[(Clarifications are in brackets after we have read the session's transcript of Mark's initial interview back for accuracy)

(Mark) I was being accused of being dishonest. Dishonest about the truths in which I told. The truths in which I told were those that I saw, those that I heard and those that I felt, those that I was around, and those that I met. For, I only spoke the truth. I only spoke the truth indeed. For, bringing these truths to the forefront and writing these truths were something, something that in essence got me killed. For, many people, many people died for telling the truth. Many people died for speaking the truth and many people died for preaching the truth. For when those of us preached the truth, preached the truth about our understanding in who God was and what God was, this is when the government would bring death upon us. Bring death upon us,

indeed. For, I was captured, captured by that which were the soldiers, the soldiers on guard.

Joseph: Were they the Jewish soldiers or Roman soldiers?

Marisa: [Inaudible.] Of course, as soon as they come in, [inaudible].

Joseph: Right. Jews weren't allowed to kill anybody. They....

(Mark) It wasn't Jewish soldiers.

Marisa: It wasn't...it seems like Roman soldiers...hold on.

(Mark) I stood upon a pillar of truth. This pillar of truth was the experiences in which I had. And when I felt the happiness, I also felt the aggression, the aggression that I felt towards words being changed, words being changed in which I spoke. For, when man begins to bring upon their own will into the words that others say, and that be as I referred to the wise man prior to that, I felt a strong sense and need to bring about, bring about the truth that was being spoken to me, and when these words were changed this brought about anger.

Marisa: So are you talking about your books that you wrote in the Bible? Wasn't the Bible written after he was dead? The Bible wasn't written while he was alive, was it?

Joseph: No. The Bible wasn't written until 300 years later.

Marisa: Yeah. He's talking about words that he preached or told.

Joseph: The Jews of course had Jesus killed because they thought of him as a threat.

Marisa: What are adversaries?

Joseph: Adversaries were probably the Sanhedrin, which was the ruling government class of the Jews (sort of like their congress).

(Mark) The adversaries were those that did not want the truth told.

Joseph: That would be the Jews. That would be the Sanhedrin and the --.

Marisa: Did not want the....he says it's not the Sanhedrin --.

Joseph: The Pharisees?

(Mark) Pharisees.

Joseph: Okay.

Marisa: He says the Pharisees.

Joseph: Yeah, the Pharisees are the ones that would take who they didn't like to the Roman governor of the town, the city that they were in for judgment. In Jesus' case they (the Jewish guards) took him, they took Jesus first to the Sanhedrin council, the Sanhedrin council of Pharisees before he was taken to Pilot, the head of the

Roman army and government in Jerusalem at the time. The Sanhedrin became the governing class of the Jews in the city.

Marisa: He's saying not Sanhedrin for some reason, but --.

Joseph: Okay. They were Pharisees. The Pharisees.

Marisa: Pharisees. Pharisees. So he says...

Joseph: The Pharisees would go to the governor, the Roman governor and say, "This guy needs to die because he's telling untruths."

Marisa: Well, yeah, that's what he's saying. He's saying that he was speaking truths and a lot of what.... he says:

(Mark) A lot of what I told, a lot of what I spoke of were things that were told to me the way that your daughter hears these things. For, many people thought that I was not right in the head. Many people thought that my prophecies (that which I told of that which would happen to Jesus) said that these things were not true. There are many that thought that the things that I saw and the things that I felt were that of witchery. There were some that heard and knew that my mother prayed to many gods. For, they felt as if some of the information coming through was from what they would say "the dark side." And for my preaching and my teachers that I brought about through the words that I wrote, some did not believe, but many things came true. This made people uneasy. For, there were many that were killed because they could see the future. There were many that were killed because they said that they

could see the future and were wrong. I saw these things and there were some people that knew this, but for the most part, this was not why I was killed, and I was not killed because I was looking over my shoulder or because I ran from the law enforcement pact or group in which I was forced to be upon. I joined in this when I learned the ministry. I joined this because I felt I had no other family. But we were forced to do things that I knew were wrong (when he was a soldier) and when I felt embraced by and loved by the group of 32 then this is where my loyalty fell upon. For, my loyalty fell upon those who loved me for who I was, who did not use me for what I could see, and did not condemn me for what I could see either. For, judgment, just as it is in today's world, is the worst feeling anyone can ever feel. For when one is judged, they know that there is nothing they can say that will change someone's mind, for the judgment has already been made. Whether being judged by a human being or being judged by the government, it does not matter. When you are judged you are condemned for being something that you may or may not be. So whether I was guilty or not guilty, I was killed for a right, a purpose, and a belief. So I will not say that this was not something that was planned in the chart in which I wrote in which I planned to go down to do, because it was.

(Jesus) (As referenced in "**Heaven Speaks**" *every soul prior to incarnation creates a life plan that is approved by Christ and is referenced to as the chart or the life chart, the plan).*

(Mark) I lived out my days and I prepared the message in which was to be told to the world. I accomplished this and I accomplished it well and now I stand on this side indeed and watch as the world can at times not

understand the words in which we are told, not understand the words in which were written, but this is okay because for the most part the message was brought across in love and light, in God, in source, and the Holy Spirit, and that which is bringing this sixth sense into the human beings to bring messages through. This is one thing that many people did not understand of me, in that many of the messages that were transpiring through the thoughts that I had were not of this world. For, I do not live in this world, nor did I live in this world prior to incarnating in this world. For, I live in other dimensions, other planets, other planetary systems, other universes, but was part of this world prior to it being the world that it is today. For many call it the lost city of Atlantis. Many call it many other things. But as a medium aged soul, I lived in the more developed world which resided on earth and learned many trades, learned how to heal, learned how to educate, and I learned the science of the earth. So when I returned for this incarnation as Mark, I came with an inner knowing and I came with the guides in which I worked with prior. I came with the high priest. I came with the scientists. I came with a minister. I came with a scholar. I came with all of these guides in which I worked with when I was on the earth plane before. So these are the wise men that I speak of. These are the wise men I speak of indeed, and these are the ones that I channeled, that I wrote with, that I dedicated my life to, and they were the ones that helped me to see what needed to be said and what needed to be done for I truly did have a strong connection with many of the people that I met and became friends with. So my message to the world was what came through in the text that you read today. It was not necessarily important where I grew up or what I did or where I went. Rather it was the message of love and light that came through, to help people to understand that a man can dedicate himself to the world and die for the sins of others and not in the sense that one man dies and everybody gets off on what they do, but to show, to show people, to show people that dying, dying does take away the sins that you lived in this lifetime, but dying, dying on a cross for some sins helps people to see that when they think life is really that bad and they are feeling greed and lust and anger and power struggle, and they are feeling all of these things that the human mind feels over things that really aren't that big of a deal, they see death as something that reminds them that... "Maybe my problems aren't that big of a deal anymore; maybe I should forgive my neighbor, maybe I should forgive my friend for at least I'm not dying." And this was kind of a reminder to the people. This was a reminder. And when this, this crucifixion happened, when Jesus quote/unquote "died for everyone's sins," it was to show that God loves us no matter what. God would die for us. And although I do not say Jesus is God, and although Jesus does not say Jesus is God, God shows that God would die for his children just as a parent would die for their children. And people must see God being merciful, not God being evil. And many people saw God as an evil god at that time. What God wanted was for people to see God as compassionate and not to be feared. For, many stories were told, many stories were told indeed, in that which is the Bible, the New Testament and the Old, whereby making God sound ruthless, evil, mean, vengeful, wrathful. And these are not any of the traits of God. These are the traits of man.]

(Back to the original taping)

Joseph: I think there is going to be a lot of wonderment to Mark because nobody really knows who Mark is. If Mark is still here, what happened between you and Paul? Was there something that happened? You and Paul were out doing ministry together and then...

Marisa: Who said they were doing ministry together?

Joseph: The Bible...Luke in the book of Acts and then eventually Paul left Mark and took off with Timothy.

Marisa: There was an alliance made.

Joseph: An alliance?

Marisa: There was an alliance made between the two of them. (This is the higher self talking.)

(Mark's higher self) There was an alliance made between the two of them and Paul felt that Mark was a lot like the government. It was a simple case of "oh well at least I'm not like that...he needs to repent for his sins". Both of them were doing the same thing to each other and were just being human beings.

Joseph: Oh, each was judging the other?

Marisa: Uh huh.

Joseph: Okay so they just had a parting of the ways.

Marisa: Yeah, they were having a male ego like.... "at least I'm not like this and at least I'm not like that." Here's Jesus:

(Jesus) The Bible says these people who wrote these books were so wise, but they were human just like anybody these days, which is the problem with the (understanding of the) Bible; which is the problem because it expresses that you need to follow the laws of the Romans at that time and stay in line with the law. This would be to say that California sets laws and then in 2000 years the entire world would have to live by the laws of California or else they are going to hell. So this is the understanding that the church brought through in order to keep people in line, to obey. The Apostles, the writers, the followers were all human obviously and had their downfalls. They had their traits of loneliness, criticism, sadness and perpetualism.

Marisa: Perpetualism? What does that mean?

Joseph: Doing the same things over and over and over again and probably expecting a better result.

Marisa: Outside, Mark is the one with the drinking problem.

Joseph: Really?

Marisa: Let me see...is it a drinking problem? Oh, no, no, no. Sorry, there is somebody right in front of me that keeps drinking something. I can't tell...

Joseph: Is he here for our highest and best? Is somebody new in the room?

Marisa: Yeah, he keeps popping in and he is like the Roman soldier guy and he is sitting there like downing like a shot or something.

Joseph: I wonder if he is the one that caught and killed Mark or maybe he was one of Mark's friends. Ask him then if he was one of Mark's friends when Mark was in the army.

Marisa: Mark, was that one of your friends? No.

Joseph: Does he know him? Ask him if he knows him.

Marisa: No, he knows of him. Okay, he needs to leave. Archangel Michael, can you please get this guy to leave? It's Abel.

Joseph: What's his name? His name is Abel?

Marisa: Abel Ontrestine or Abel Ostrestine of the... like family or something. He decided when he was 4 years old that he wanted to grow up and be a soldier. He was one of the ones that would seek out and find people but he was not the one that caught Jesus. Somehow he ended up in here (this taped session on Mark). When we were talking about the soldiers that is when he came in.

Joseph: So Abel is one of the soldiers that either was with Mark in the army or he was a soldier that...

Marisa: No it is just a ghost. Just a ghost of a soldier and I made him go away. Somewhere in our mind obviously we called in a Roman soldier.

Joseph: Oh, gosh. Okay, we don't need the Roman soldier in here.

Marisa: Yeah I know. Okay, let's see, Abraham can you remove him please. Take him back home and please reseal the room.

Joseph: Let's get back into the recap. Let's see if Mark has got anything else he wants to add. I think we've got a pretty good idea...his wife had a very hard life and...

(Mark) ...everybody's life is hard. Everybody has the indifference to one side or the other. Life was black or white in that time. You could still say that living in a certain conscious level the world is still black or white, but what you are doing in bringing this forward, as Yeshua has explained it to me, is you are trying to bring the adversity in the world into a union of friendship of each. I brought more conspiracy through the writings in which I did because I like to get down to the core or the root of things and gladly wrote in these books...

Marisa's dog Poochie: (Growling sound)

Marisa: Oh darn, that Roman soldier. Is this still Mark? Yes. Okay, it says here... (Growling sound) Go away.

Joseph: Somebody is here, right?

Marisa: I know...it's a blue chief getting upset. Okay, let's see here.

Joseph: Jesus, could you please clear the room? Could Jesus please just clear out anybody who doesn't belong here?

Marisa: I've asked him and he never clears the room completely. I don't understand why.

Joseph: Because he's got such a kind heart. He probably believes in everybody.

Marisa: He just sends light and that's like thanks.

Joseph: So people are attracted to his light?

Marisa: Yes.

Joseph: They are coming in because of his light? or your light?

Marisa: I hope they are not coming in to try to trick us.

[(Note from Jesus to Joe) Lost souls are attracted to my light and I help them get to heaven and so sometimes during these sessions random souls seek me out for help and every once in a while the channel (Marisa) can see them. This is why they appear when you've asked me to clear the room. They're just seeking me out for help while I happen to be helping with these interviews).]

Joseph: I don't want to be tricked. We'll make sure that everything that we have in here is correct.

Marisa: Yeah.

Joseph: Now please...

Marisa: Calling in Archangel Michael and your legion of angels to sweep through this house; every nook and cranny in every dimension, the ones that we know of and the ones that we don't. Please sweep through every aspect of our being, past, present and future within each dimension and remove anything that doesn't belong. Please connect me St. Germaine with these beings that I need to channel and help to regulate the energy so that I am not so tired when I connect with them because of their vibration. We ask that you do this now. Thank you. Okay so Jesus is now looking very young. His hair is short. He always comes in with blue eyes.

Joseph: *That is what Rosemary said. She said he was cute. She said he had long hair and a beard but he cut it off in the summertime but it was his eyes.*

Marisa: *Yeah, his eyes are like magical.*

Joseph: *Like charisma. I think I've described it to people, as I've explained to people what I'm learning and hearing from Jesus and those who followed him is that his charisma is off the charts. Jesus will never call it that himself. That is what I'm going to try to get out of all of these interviews and what their take is.*

(Jesus) I came into a body and I came into a mind that would understand that free will was a key, but understand that personality is one of the most important things while in any egoic run body for if one has the best personality in the world they may tell lies and others will believe them. If somebody has no personality at all they may tell truths and nobody will listen to them. So knowing that, the people in whom I would be born into I knew that there must be a charismatic nature to that human being which I lived in. So yes I will admit to the charisma as a positive attribute to the ministry for if there was no charisma there is no charm as you would say in

these days. There would not have been such an impact for people who are attracted to the light, and what I brought forth was for them to understand not to worship me but to worship the God inside each and every one of us. And this was the teachings in which I brought. But human beings, just as they have done for millions and millions of years, tend to worship their fellow brothers and sisters if they are further along their path than others. This would be like first graders in elementary school worshipping a sixth grader because they passed school. When really they are just a fellow student and they are not any worse than the sixth grader, they are just younger. So know that when I brought this information through to the writers of the Bible, when I brought the information through to the ceremonious events that would occur, people needed to see what being influenced by spirit or of the spirit would do for a human existence, for if people were trained today, they could do exactly the same things that I was able to do and more, for the Earth carried a lower vibration at that time, and it was much harder back then to access the higher vibration spirit, the holy spirit, the soul's consciousness, and all the way up. So know that it was very important that I was not to be worshipped because that takes the glory from God.

Joseph: In one passage that is in a number of the (Bible) books, primarily John.....I will get into that when we get into our interview with John...they have asked...your disciples asked you; had you seen the father? Had you met the father? Of course I'm paraphrasing here. And your response was...as you see me you see the father. And again I am paraphrasing. So you taught them that you were not God but that by accepting you they were seeing the father.

(Jesus) Each one of us is God and as the consciousness raises there are more of the attributes that come whereby if one, if one is spiritually young just as we have said in first grade they will not see the positive influence they can have using the power of God within each of us. You must understand that the church had to make a martyr out of someone so the people would feel guilty enough to worship and repent. This is something that is completely off the subject but at the same time very on the subject in that yes, the Holy Spirit resides within each person. Yes, each person is a human soul living in a physical body. Yes, I taught how to in the terms of what the channel may use, raise the vibration of the human existence whereby to pray, channel, and directly communicate with the Godhead within each of us and this was taught to the followers, the 32, and they were able to communicate with that which was their higher self or that which was the Holy Spirit. And this is what I taught. This is what I taught to teach each person that they can do just as I did and more. And when the church came to write these things, many things, when the church came in many things were changed. So understand that the understanding of God within each of us was that which when you open your heart to God, when you release your sins, when you allow yourself to feel the Holy Spirit you will become more God-like, more Christ-like and this is why I came down to teach this for I have lived through millions of years of a very old soul evolved through third dimensional worlds into Christhood and could not just sit on the other side watching as human beings killed each other; for I came into this life with an understanding that I was going to change the world, and this has happened. My guides helped me through, my soul family members, and to the humans at that time, even to the humans at this time, the abilities I had, which anyone can have with the persistence of working with spirit and releasing just as I

have said, releasing the negativity about oneself and sins so to speak can become just like the way that I as spirit was residing in a physical body. Does this make sense?

Joseph: It makes sense. The one thing I question is, Jesus you say that everyone can do what you can do and you taught them.

(Jesus) What they are taught is to understand and bring in that worthiness for when one believes I have talents that have not surfaced they will have more faith within themselves, and more of an understanding that they will want to move forward in utilizing these gifts. They may not be a master even before they die, but the recognition of knowing that the Holy Spirit and the abilities of Christ are within each person helps to allow them to love themselves.

Joseph: If you only need to have the faith that the Holy Spirit is there for them all the way, all the time and that they need to learn to love themselves....

(Jesus) Yes, not by pointing a finger saying, at least I'm not them, or at least I'm not like that. This is not the road to enlightenment.

Marisa: Let me see...

Joseph: Yeah I just thought of what you taught; before you take the speck out of your neighbor's eye first take the plank out of yours. In other words someone shouldn't be criticizing that person because what he's doing is even worse!

(Jesus) But it's human nature and that is what humans do, and this is the whole divine creation and the

experiment on this planet where divine human souls just as yourself can incarnate into a world that is run by selfish greed and understanding between light and dark where many will take dark because it is more fun, but being a soul that incarnates into these animalistic creatures is something that is quite a challenge and a blessing. I owe all of this to those who believed. If none had believed then nothing would have happened after I left. I left for many years (while living as a human) and trained my emotional, mental and spiritual bodies so that when I returned to the town in which I was born I would be able to teach other people.

Marisa: He is saying India.

Joseph: Yeah, when I interview you Jesus for the last book in this series of Authors I'm going to ask you about your life that isn't portrayed in the Bible. You know, where were you? Where did you go? What did you learn? Who did you commune with? etc. It is not the time yet because I do want to do my other interviews first and finish up with you Jesus for your own book, but even though I know you can keep an eye on the Earth right now....but....boy, Christianity is under assault everywhere. Everywhere around the world there is evil that is killing Christians and even then there are secularists that just continue to make fun of Christians now. I hope our Pope is going to come out and help. That is all I can say and I do not want to detract from the Bible. There have been a couple of times in these conversations that you said "the problem with", or something to the effect, "with the Bible is...; and I don't want to use words like that. I don't want to say "the problem with the Bible is" because I don't want to doubt the Bible.....

(Jesus) This is why many of the conversations in which we carry are not so much confidential but we are sharing this information with you to share with the world. So in using word for word, many of the things that we say, this is not good, but you must understand in order for you to write something, if you do not understand the whole truth you are only writing a half-truth thinking it is the whole-truth. So we tell it all.

Joseph: I keep hearing your words. I know you don't want me to detract from the Bible and we don't want to go negative. You said otherwise you are going to "shut it (these conversations) down". So I don't want to shut it down. I don't want you to shut this down. I just want to put out the book you want us to put out. I'm going to do the best I can. Marisa, God bless her that she can talk to all of you guys, is just so amazing.

(Jesus) This is a blessing for us as well to keep the memory alive and to keep the faith strong on the planet for we have chosen as Masters and as Christed beings to remain in the realms of the human beings. Many have traveled to other planets. Other universes began to create their own worlds but there are many of us who stayed behind to help the human beings on earth to evolve for we cherish the human beings. We love the human beings.

Joseph: We love you too Christ. Jesus we love you.

(Jesus) And I was a man walking and living the temptations and the rule of the egoic mind, the intellectual mind over the spirit so I can relate to those on the Earth-plane at this time. For again I am not just an idol to be worshipped, I am someone who may be called on at any time just as we have spoken about

already though in one of the other books of this series...the last time we spoke. See me as a minister speaking through a microphone, and as each person tunes in to this ministry whether they are listening or not, their subconscious mind will hear it, and this will raise their vibration, and the negativity will fall off. They will forget that there is negativity even on them and they will become believers. So this is a constant battle so to speak getting the human beings to understand. The same story has to be used over and over and over again in history and that is because human beings want to believe.

Joseph: I'm just blown away that we get to talk to you. I mean every Pastor, every Priest; everybody who loves you Lord would love to have a conversation with you. I know, I wasn't going to say why us because you get irritated when I say that...

(Jesus) The conversations in which we have with each person on this planet are a conversation in which they receive. They just may not consciously receive this. Many receive it in dreams. Many receive it through messages throughout the day. As one has explained in the past you may have looked at every message in which we send to each field as a message left in their field written on a little piece of paper. As this little piece of paper flies around and runs into the head, the head will then say, I know what I need to do, and this is because we've been delivering these messages.

Joseph: I feel that.

(Jesus) There are many people that feel that the channel and the other channels are not sufficient to do this while still believing in what I stand for and this is something that is going to be changed.

Joseph: Something is going to be changed? Well we can't do prophecy. Everybody wants to know when Jesus is coming again but I don't want to ask the questions now. I don't want an answer.

Marisa: He is already here.

Joseph: I know but everybody is waiting for another David. They want to see a big strong Jesus with holes in his hands and holes in his feet and a hole in his side from a spear.

Marisa: Why?

Joseph: I don't know.

Marisa: As proof?

Joseph: Yes. They want Jesus to come and wipe out everybody that doesn't believe in Christ.

Marisa: That will never happen.

Joseph: No, because Christians believe that... In John 14:6 it says Jesus that you are the way, the truth and the light... It is said that Jesus said: "I am the way, the truth, and the light and no one gets to the father but through me." So Christians believe that anybody who does not believe in you will go to hell and I think they are waiting for the day you are going to come to the Earth and you are going to wipe out all those people who don't believe in you and leave a paradise for the remaining Christians. I just kind of wag my head...

(Jesus) It is absolutely not true in that it brings in an understanding that we are judgmental on this side. We may have judged in the human bodies in which we lived, but who says that one believes or does not really believe? There are many more than 70% of the Christians today that don't really believe. Their ego believes but their intellectual mind does not. Their spirit wants to believe but it doesn't understand it. So 70% of these church goers that do not believe are in worse off shape than those that don't believe that don't go to church because there is a contradiction going on, a frustration when one does not believe because they do not understand. So as we bring in the information that we bring through to you and to many other channels, the things that are expressed are things that add knowledge to teachings and the understandings of that which was the past. There are so many that already shamed the Bible. There are so many that say this (the Bible) is not God's word. They say this is man's word which we do not totally disagree with. But it is the understanding that we are here to acknowledge what was written as a historical paper, a historical writing and an understanding of who God is so when I say that you must go through me to get to the father, I spoke of the Christ.

Joseph: Right and that is what I wrote about in my newspaper article last week.

Marisa: You did?

Joseph: Yeah, eventually you'll read it, but eventually yeah everybody has to go through Christ to get to the father because that is the last stop because Christ lives with the Father.

(Jesus) And again, you look at it as people, in the place....and we can get back into the dimensions and planes and levels another time, but you must look at this as a source or a database. The only human thing about this information and consciousness is the human consciousness that is created in order to incarnate into a human being. So when one is connecting with Christ they don't necessarily need to go somewhere. They just must understand that Christ is the light. But one may go directly to the father as well in the understanding that you may become your own God, that you may become a creator of your own but you must become Christed first as I did and then move on from there.

Joseph: That must take an awful long time.

Marisa: About 2 million years.

Joseph: Ha, ha, ha. Well eternity is a long time. Well, I'd love to continue getting all these great words from Jesus but I really do want to do the full interview for our last book in the Authors series so I think what we have is...

Marisa: We're done with Mark. He is already gone.

Joseph: He is gone. Okay. Mark came in... I was going to ask if Mark had anything else to say.

Marisa: No, he's gone.

Joseph: And Jesus wrapped that up. Mark did his summary then Jesus came in and kind of put a punctuation mark on it. Rosemary is still here and I do like Rosemary's take. So if Rosemary can give us...she obviously knew Mark also. You Rosemary, tell us what your take on Mark was? What kind of person was he?

(Rosemary) He always seemed very deceptive. He always seemed like he was hiding something or lying or cheating and this is something that he had on his face because he was always trying to hide or rebel or try to understand why people do what they do. So he was constantly looking to see if somebody was there to hurt him. So other people took this offensively in defense of this and became defensive.

Joseph: Well, he was an AWOL soldier.

(Rosemary) Exactly, but nobody knew this. People did not know this and they knew that there was a man that was following the group and he would sometimes stay with them and other times he would stay at other places. He was very mysterious and he would listen to the stories and tell these stories, and he had those who would help him write the stories, but this was just something that did not define him at the time. It just happened that these books ended up in what human beings call a Bible. If people were here at this time during the, as they say "Bible times", where spirit was free-flowing from the other side, for I communicated with my higher self the entire time on the Earth-plane, just as everybody communicates with their higher self, they just do not realize it. They don't realize it. So when Jesus says to go within, to go within the Christ to get to the Father, what he is saying is everybody has a piece inside of them that is Christ and everybody, because there is not time in certain dimensions, everybody has already become Christed. Just as you two sit right now, the outer layers of your body are 34 thousand years in your future and they are becoming Christed.

Joseph: Whoa.

(Rosemary) So this is something that is hard to wrap a human mind around and this is something I surely would not have understood while in a human body, but if you look at it this way and look at time as non-existent you'll see that you can actually pull information from the you that is living thousands of years ahead of you and you may pull that information into your daily life. So this is what Jesus taught. He taught us to go to the aspect of ourselves that's inside of ourselves, that piece of God, that piece of Christ within us, for without that piece of understanding we are unable to fully become Christed beings and we are fully unable to proceed without this to become like God. For the vibration that needs to be carried in order to directly hear the God-head needs to be fairly high and not very many human beings are capable of doing that. But more and more of these days, I've been told, there are people that understand this and need to be educated more otherwise they will think they are crazy or bad or evil.

Joseph: Maybe our book line will end up helping those people.

Marisa: I would love to help those people. She is funny. So are you a guide Rosemary?

(Rosemary) Yes I am a Spirit Guide in one aspect of myself in one dimension.

Marisa: So how old are our souls? 86,400 (years). Is that our souls, our spirits, or our higher selves? She just goes:

(Rosemary) Oh you just make it so complicated."

Joseph: Ha, ha, ha.

(Rosemary) Just look at the spirit, or the soul or the higher self as the higher piece of you and understand that within that piece of you imagine a tennis ball cut in half and that tennis ball inside of it has a smaller tennis ball that fits perfectly in it. So there is a little rim inside and then another smaller tennis ball and another smaller tennis ball and then a small and small and smaller all the way down. If you look at that as your higher self, your spirit, your soul for each layer, if you look at that as the Christ within you, this covers everything and this is what Jesus taught.

Joseph: Oh, that is nice and easy.

(Rosemary) If you look at this, look at every single aspect. For when you ask, I heard earlier when you asked, when am I able to talk to my soul? You can talk to your soul right now. You can talk to your soul. You can talk to your soul group, you can talk to your over-soul, you can talk to Christ and you can talk to God whether you can hear them back, that is a different story. We are much easier to hear as we have incarnated as guides and we are easier to hear at times than words directly from God. But God sends these messages with angels. With angels many a time, so you will get the messages regardless. But please look at that piece of God inside of you. It is a multi-layered ball and when you utilize that you do not need to differentiate between, I'm calling my spirit, I'm calling my higher self, I'm calling my soul, oh wait no, no, I need to call in Christ or wake the over-soul!

Marisa: She's being exuberant. She is making fun of it (how we pray).

Joseph: Ha, ha, ha. That is okay. I don't mind.

(Rosemary) Well what we need to do is to understand that all of these levels are God and you are God just as I am God, but I understand that Eden just said, "You know what Rosemary, they need to understand it that way otherwise they are not going to understand. (Eden is one of Joseph's guides)

Marisa: Eden is getting all... not defensive, but just kind of like...

(Rosemary) It may have been easy for you to understand when you are there because the consciousness was lower to just go okay God, but Eden is saying that there are a lot of people on the Earth-plane right now that need to understand the hierarchy because they will understand how they were created and where they came from.

Joseph: Well we did the foundation in our first book I think.

Marisa: Yeah.

Joseph: I mean it is not a perfect book, but the foundation is there.

Marisa: Yeah, the book is good.

Joseph: I know, I don't want any negativity in this at all.

(Eden) There won't be any negativity but we must share with you the exact information so that you may

understand how to place the information so that it is correct, but not negative for we do not want to draw any Christians, true Christians away from Christianity. But there will be a world with no religion in the near future. Within the next few hundred years, religion will not exist. Religion is laws. Religion is government. Religion is power, control and undermining the human being of what they are capable of. And assigning people who are Godlier than another because they say they are and having people go to that person in order to connect with God when God is as Rosemary said a tennis ball surrounded by another tennis ball and another tennis ball inside, in layers like an onion and when that piece of God inside is resonated with and spoken to it speaks back. For do not look at God as outside of you, look at God as something somewhere everywhere and the inside of that tennis ball has a walkie-talkie, and this walkie-talkie communicates directly with God wherever God may be. So technically, listening to the inside of you is where you are getting the information, not from the outside, so this must be understood as well and as soon as people can understand that God does not judge, you do not need to go to another human being in order to connect with God, the world will be a completely different place, and this is what we look forward to.

Marisa: Whoa, where am I? What did she say?

Joseph: I think we are wrapped up. We've been doing this for about 2 hours and 45 minutes.

Marisa: Whoa. Oh my God. I want to ask them a question really quick. It is 12:12.

Joseph: Yeah, its 12:12.

Marisa: I always look at the clock at...

Joseph: I know those numbers. We are already communicating with them right now.

Marisa: Okay Abraham, how about Sarah, "Can you come in here please?" Okay Sarah, I have a question for you. The writer Elizabeth Clare Prophet is an author. She's a channel and a medium. So do you know who she is?

(Sarah) Yes, she was a messenger of St. Germaine. First she came from the ray in which St. Germaine ruled over. Much of the information in which she brought in was direct line communication with us masters but much of it was also skewed by her belief systems and the things that she had read and the things that she was raised with. So always ask, always ask with precaution when reading others' books to ask if this is truly correct. But if this is something that you are not teaching the others and you are using for yourself then the intention of connecting with somebody who may or may not have been incarnated in another it is okay because the intention is there.

Marisa: So Sarah, were you Mary Magdalene?

(Sarah) Yes.

Marisa: Was Mary Magdalene you?

(Sarah) No.

Marisa: Okay, so Sarah was first. Sarah, did you have spiritual abilities?

(Sarah) No her husband did. He spoke tongues.

Joseph: Abraham was Sarah's husband and he spoke in tongues?

(Sarah) (To Marisa) He was a channel just like you dear one. So as you evolve and move forward in your spiritual past task, please understand that the great teachers of the past have the same abilities as you and there are many on this planet that have the exact same abilities that have never uncovered them due to fear of dis-appreciation, defamation and extortion of that which is the information that they hold dear to them. So please begin to work more with your angels, do your daily meditations, and call me in. I am helping you to release the past. I am helping you to remove the residue that you have in the emotional body whereby attracting those that can harm you. We open up the third eye and we open up your sight and we open up your ability to channel to the higher dimension so do not be fearful and do not be ashamed if you cannot connect with the lower plane. This is not necessary, for you have come to connect with the higher planes of existence thereby bringing the light into the world whereby even if you were not to speak and yet stand next to somebody, you'll be raising their vibration and they will raise another, for you are here on a mission that things are changing. The gifts are evolving and growing and as you become appreciative of this, things will begin to open even more.

Marisa: Was Mary Magdalene one of the Apostles?

(Sarah) No.

Marisa: Did she hang out with them?

(Sarah) Yes. I as Mary Magdalene was an author using scribes or writers but I also learned to write for I came into the world as having a speckle of genius which caused many to think that I was crazy, thereby banning me from certain groups and certain societal aspects of living as a human being to joining the group enjoining with Christ, Lord Jesus and combining our efforts into healing the planet. We still continue to do the same together from this side. So calling in the divine feminine/the Holy Spirit of that which I stand for is something that will grow the channeling sessions into much more, for in him utilizing my energy and mine his, is just the same as you and your father utilizing the feminine and the masculine energy in connecting with that which is unseen.

Just as I thought, anything that draws negativity to Christ, Jesus or the bible does not belong in here. At the end of the tape with Mark there was some discussion about Matthew's brother sneaking into the session and bringing us four minutes of information that doesn't belong. We went back over that tape, found the information that didn't belong in there and it was removed. Jesus came right out and said that the Bible was written by men but that it was the most correct depiction of the Father that could possibly be put into a book. He said that you have to take the Bible in its entirety to understand its significance to mankind. He also said that the Bible has a spirit of its own.

So, whenever you have read in here that something is disappointing or negative about the Bible, it is not being negative. It may just be thoughts of the Authors that they wish that more of what they wrote was put into the bible or that over time the stories hadn't become a little skewed. But nonetheless, the Bible is the word of God as inspired by God to those who chose to write down what their understanding of God was/is. That's all. So don't think that when there is a word askew here or there in reference to the Authors, Jesus or the Bible that that must be Lucifer sticking his nose in this trying to dissuade anyone from the love of the Father or the Son. We'll catch it and discuss it further with our Higher Selves, our Guides and even Jesus to make sure what you are reading in these pages are the inspiration that Jesus hopes for and not a detraction.

Now we move on to Peter and John for Book II. Typically you would assume that the next two should be Luke and John but there is a reason putting Peter and John together as they were both original Apostles. Luke and Paul on the other hand were not Apostles walking with Jesus so their takes will be different than the original Apostle/Authors.

Luke and Paul will be featured in Book III in the Conversations with Jesus and the New Testament Authors series. Luke and Paul are very interesting characters as you'll see but I know you're going to love getting to know John and Peter first and when you speak of characters!!....well, keep reading!

And in conclusion of Matthew and Mark..., well, no one needs my take... You've all made up your own minds already and made conclusions so let's skip my analysis and just move on... You're going to love Peter!!! John is ..., well..., he is so intelligent!!!

Author Page

Joe, Marisa and Poochi

Joseph P. Moris is an author and columnist. Joe co-authored with his daughter Marisa their first book entitled: "Answers: Heaven Speaks." Joe also writes a lifestyle column for the North Coastal San Diego County newspaper "The Coast News" and is currently a semi-retired real estate broker/owner for Coastal Country Real Estate in Encinitas, CA and living part-time in Puerto Vallarta Mexico. Joe also studied and earned Bachelor Degrees in Political Science and Economics at the University of California, Santa Barbara.

Marisa P. Moris is the founder of *The Intuition Center* (*www.discoverintuition.com*). Marisa co-authored, with her father Joe, "Answers: *Heaven Speaks.*" She is an Intuitive Reiki Master teacher, clairvoyant, and channel who's passion it is to help people, through her classes and healing sessions, to connect with their higher self and God; to heal their lives and discover their intuition.

www.ingramcontent.com/pod-product-compliance
Lightning Source LLC
Chambersburg PA
CBHW070156100426
42743CB00013B/2937